Financing Entrepreneurs

Financing
Entrepreneurs

Edited by Cynthia A. Beltz

The AEI Press

Publisher for the American Enterprise Institute
WASHINGTON, D.C.

1994

Distributed to the Trade by National Book Network, 15200 NBN Way, Blue Ridge Summit, PA 17214. To order call toll free 1-800-462-6420 or 1-717-794-3800. For all other inquiries please contact the AEI Press, 1150 Seventeenth Street, N.W., Washington, D.C. 20036 or call 1-800-862-5801.

Library of Congress Cataloging-in-Publication Data

Financing entrepreneurs / edited by Cynthia A. Beltz.
  p. cm.
  ISBN 0-8447-3849-2
  1. Venture capital—Government policy—United States.
  2. Public investments—Government policy—United States.
  3. Industry and state—United States. 4. Technological
  innovations—Finance—Government policy—United States.
  5. New business enterprises—Finance—Government policy—
  United States. 6. High technology industries—Finance—
  Government policy—United States. I. Beltz, Cynthia A.
  HG4751.F56   1993
  332'.0415'0973—dc20   93-42531
                                                                CIP
  ISBN 978-0-8447-3849-9

1 2 3 4 5 6 7 8 9 10

THE AEI PRESS
Publisher for the American Enterprise Institute
1150 Seventeenth Street, N.W.
Washington, D.C. 20036

Contents

vi

Preface

If two inventors in the 1970s could take a good idea from a California garage workshop and turn it into one of the world's most successful computer companies, could the same thing happen today? This question is at the heart of the debate over U.S. competitiveness and the health of the entrepreneurial community. At issue is whether the financing needed for the next generation of entrepreneurs has dried up and whether taxpayer-backed alternatives to private financing are now needed to fill the capital gap.

The fate of American entrepreneurs matters because, in the minds of many, the essence of our brand of capitalism is at stake. The pioneering spirit has long been honored in the United States not only for producing innovations but also for continually rejuvenating an intricate network of wealth and jobs. The story of Apple Computer is the model: take the risk, create a revolutionary product, attract some investors, hire some employees, make a few sales, develop a network of customers and suppliers—and the company expands, the network grows, new companies spin off, and tens of thousands of jobs are created. The system works and is the source of envy around the world. But it is not indestructible.

Those who believe that there are serious deficiencies in the private capital markets which threaten the system are advancing a number of proposals, including government-created enterprises, loan guarantees for start-ups, and special tax incentives for small, high-growth firms, as well as venture capital programs in federal agencies such as the Commerce Department or the Small Business Administration.

Critics of such proposals counter that America has a healthy and dynamic system for financing entrepreneurs, which is responsible for the strong performance of high-risk, long-term horizon start-ups and emerging industries such as cellular communications. If something must be done, they argue that reducing—not increasing—the tax and regulatory burdens on firms and individual investors would more effectively stimulate investment than would any federal capital program.

On April 15, 1993, the American Enterprise Institute brought together both to explore two questions: what, if anything, is wrong with the capital market for entrepreneurial firms, and what is the government role in venture capital? The result was a spirited and provocative debate on the key assumptions underlying the push—past and present—for a federal venture capital program.

The panel, moderated by William Haraf, director of policy analysis at Citibank, included Anthony Clark, on the professional staff of the House Science Committee and the primary staff member on the venture capital provision in the 1993 National Competitiveness Act; Richard Florida of Carnegie Mellon University and author of studies on economic development and venture capital; and William Sahlman from the Harvard Business School, who has done extensive field research and produced over twenty studies on the venture capital market.

The latest effort to make government into a venture capitalist is the 1993 National Competitiveness Act (H.R. 820, S.4), which has been stopped by turf battles and legislative gridlock in the Senate. But the debate—like the larger competitiveness policy debate—will no doubt continue and perhaps even take into full account the evidence and the spectrum of views on market trends. Toward that end, this publication contributes a brief history of the policy debate, a statistical overview of the venture capital market, and a compendium of the views and insights presented at the AEI conference.

AEI is grateful for the generous support from the Sloan Foundation for this project. The editor would also like to gratefully acknowledge both the invaluable assistance of AEI's librarian, Evelyn Caldwell, and the insights of Claude Barfield, Allan Meltzer, and Mark DeSantis that helped to make the conference possible.

CYNTHIA A. BELTZ

.

Contributors

CYNTHIA A. BELTZ is a technology policy analyst at the American Enterprise Institute. Her recent publication is entitled *High Tech Maneuvers: The Industrial Policy Lessons of HDTV.* Her articles on technology and trade policy have appeared in the *New York Times,* the *Los Angeles Times,* the *Washington Times,* the *Journal of Commerce, Reason Magazine, Regulation,* and *The American Enterprise.* She has recently testified before the House Budget and Science committees on American living standards and the problems of high-tech targeting. In addition, she organized and participated in AEI conferences on defense R&D institutions after the cold war, industrial policy, and the government's role in the venture capital market. She is now writing a monograph on technology jobs and economic security.

ANTHONY S. CLARK is a professional staff member on the House Committee on Science, Space, and Technology. Mr. Clark assists in developing legislation pertaining to U.S. technology policy, economic development, industrial competitiveness, and investment in infrastructure technologies. He was the lead staffer on the technology financing titles of the National Competitiveness Act of 1993 and is responsible for staff oversight of the technology programs of the Department of Commerce. Before joining the congressional staff in 1991, Mr. Clark was vice president of Wheat, First Securities, Inc., in Richmond, Virginia.

RICHARD FLORIDA is associate professor of management and public policy in the H. John Heinz III School of Public Policy and Management and in the Department of Engineering and Public Policy at Carnegie Mellon University. He is currently leading studies of venture capital and industrial competitiveness. Mr. Florida is a consultant and adviser to multinational business and government agencies in the United States and Japan. Before coming to Carnegie Mellon University, Mr. Florida was on the faculty of Ohio State University. His latest book is *Beyond Mass Production: The Japanese System and Its Transfer to the U.S.* (Oxford Press, 1993).

WILLIAM S. HARAF is vice president for policy analysis with Citicorp in Washington, D.C., where he is responsible for analyzing a broad range of public policy issues affecting Citicorp and the financial industry. In addition, Mr. Haraf is a member of the Economic Advisory Committee for the U.S. Chamber of Commerce and of the Economic Policy Committee of the American Bankers Association. Before joining Citicorp in 1989, Mr. Haraf was the J. Edward Lundy Scholar and director of the Financial Markets Project at the American Enterprise Institute. He is a coeditor of *Restructuring Banking and Financial Services in America* (AEI Press, 1989).

WILLIAM A. SAHLMAN is the Dimitri V. d'Arbeloff–Class of 1955 Professor of Business Administration at Harvard Business School. His research focuses on the in-

vestment and financing decisions made in entrepreneurial ventures at all stages in their development. Related lines of research include the role of financial institutions in providing risk capital and the role of government policy in influencing capital formation in the
entrepreneurial sector of the economy. Mr. Sahlman is
senior associate dean, director of publishing activities
at Harvard Business School. His article "Insights from
the American Venture Capital Industry" was published
as part of the Harvard Business School and Council on
Competitiveness study of time horizons in business.

ONE

Introduction
Cynthia A. Beltz

President Clinton entered the White House with a promise to make the government a direct and active partner in the development of advanced technologies. Many were quick to take him up on the offer. In venture capital, direct federal financing of entrepreneurial firms is once again being touted as a tool to restore U.S. high-tech competitiveness. Take, for example, the recent recommendations of the Competitiveness Policy Council, an advisory committee created by Congress, that government agencies such as the Advanced Research Projects Agency (ARPA) (formerly DARPA), the Department of Commerce, and the National Institutes of Health be allowed to make investments in start-ups both directly or through a government-created technology bank.[1] The bank would work with existing financial institutions and use equity, loans, or loan guarantees to support commercialization of new ideas.

---

[1]Competitiveness Policy Council, *Reports of the Subcouncils: A Competitiveness Strategy for America* (Washington, D.C.: Free Hand Press, March 1, 1993), p. 116.

1

Reviving Old Ideas

Neither proposal is new. Instead, both resurrect ideas rejected during the often heated industrial policy debate under the Bush administration. In April 1990, for example, the active promotion of direct government investment in fledgling high-tech companies cost DARPA director Craig Fields his job. The problems started in 1989 when Fields ignored the official "just say no" Bush line on industrial policy and promoted before congressional committees the case for a government high-definition television (HDTV) program. The willingness of the Bush administration to tolerate such public displays of dissent ended a year later when Fields decided to invest $4 million in a Silicon Valley maker of gallium arsenide chips (Gazelle Microcircuits), which entitled DARPA to cash payments or royalties on products developed by the company. As Arati Prabhakar,[2] program manager for the Gazelle project, put it to the *New York Times,* "From the company's point of view, we look an awful lot like a regular investor."[3] Unfortunately for Fields, from the Bush White House's point of view, the government should not be in the business of making commercial investments.[4]

---

[2]Arati Prabhakar is now director of the National Institute of Standards and Technology.

[3]Andrew Pollack, "Silicon Valley Investment by Pentagon," *New York Times,* April 10, 1990.

[4]In times past, the government through the Defense Department has arguably played the role of venture capitalist, nurturing those technologies believed to be essential to America's defense industrial base. But in the realm of commercial affairs, the government is in a completely different ballgame with different objectives, rules, and constraints. The government is neither the principal customer nor the

2

Unwilling to concede defeat, when the direct approach did not work, federal activists pushed for quasi-independent government organizations or technology corporations. In the midst of the HDTV debate, the National Advisory Committee (NAC) on Semiconductors put forward a proposal for a government-backed fund for risky electronics projects—the Electronics Capital Corporation (ECC): "The linchpin of ECC is a multi-billion dollar pool of patient, low-cost capital available to established, as well as start-up, companies willing to enter the market for high volume electronics. . . . As an investor, ECC would operate its own venture fund and act as lead or participant in other investor consortia." As a lender, the ECC would use its own funds to limit foreign purchases of U.S. companies in critical industries.[5] The ECC would raise equity from institutions and state and local governments that would then be backed by government guarantees or "pledges of support" to lower the effective cost of capital.[6]

Government support of course comes tied in strings. At a minimum, the NAC report recommended that an

---

commander of the economy. To project past experience in defense onto a government role in commercial affairs is therefore akin to mixing apples and oranges.

[5]In response to questions about the Electronics Capital Corporation from its first report, *A Strategic Industry at Risk* (Washington, D.C., November 1989), the National Advisory Committee on Semiconductors provided a more detailed report, *Electronics Capital Corporation* (Washington, D.C., July 1990), from which the details in the text are taken, especially pp. 2–3.

[6]For the financial impact on ECC of government support, see Michael Borrus, "The Electronics Capital Consortium," working paper submitted to the National Advisory Committee on Semiconductors, May 1990, p. 3.

ECC be audited once a year to ensure that it meets its obligations and provides fair returns to investors and the public. Many in the business community balked at such oversight and direction. In particular, Arthur Rock, a prominent venture capitalist, strongly objected to an ECC because he viewed the fast-charging, complex business of high-tech investment as incompatible with a committee hindered by government regulations.[7] As a result of internal committee disputes and the opposition of the Bush administration, the ECC proposal was dead on arrival in Washington.

Similar fates greeted two versions of the ECC proposal that appeared in 1990 and 1992.[8] First, the federally chartered Technology Corporation of America was proposed by Congressman Mel Levine (D-Calif.) to act as a catalyst for developing high-tech start-ups in advanced technologies and industries. The corporation would be financed by direct federal funding for research and development (R&D) and manufacturing that would be matched by extensive federal oversight: government officials would participate on and appoint

[7]NAC, *Toward a National Semiconductor Strategy*, second annual report, vol. 1, Feb. 1991, p. 45. Ian Ross, president of AT&T's Bell Laboratories and chairman of the committee, argued that ECC was also scrapped in the NAC second annual report because the committee could not design a way for the idea to work. Valerie Rice, "Group Proposes New Initiative," *Electronic Business,* April 8, 1991, p. 13.

[8]Both versions are based on a background paper on the ECC that presented three different options to the NAC for how government participation in an ECC could be structured. Levine's bill closely resembles the full participation model, while the Rockefeller version promoted limited government participation. See Borrus, "The Electronics Capital Consortium."

most members of the board of directors; in addition, an annual report and audit would be required for congressional review.[9]

Then in 1992, Senator Jay Rockefeller (D-W.Va.) proposed his version of the ECC—the Advanced Technologies Capital Consortium (ATCC)—a $500 million federal venture capital program sponsored by the Department of Commerce and advised by a government-industry committee. He argued that the "venture capital market failed to provide sufficient funds to support innovation or commercialization of critical technologies."[10] Lamenting the fall in the venture capital market after 1987, Senator Rockefeller concluded that the government needed to offset the "growing deficiencies in the domestic venture capital market" and provide a "domestic venture capital alternative." But like its step-sisters, the ECC and the Levine proposal, the ATCC initiative died in committee and never got off the ground.

H.R. 820 and Congressional Gridlock. Under the Clinton administration, where industrial policy is looked on more favorably, a provision in the proposed National Competitiveness Act of 1993 (H.R. 820, S. 4) would move the government further into the venture capital business through a program housed in the Department of Commerce. (For a history of venture capital–related legislation, see appendixes A and B.) The under secretary would act much like a general or senior partner: selecting and licensing the participating venture capital firms and directing their investment of

---

[9]H.R. 4715, 101st Congress, 2d session, May 2, 1990.

[10]S. 2286 (Advanced Technologies Capital Consortium Act of 1992), Section 2(a)(6), 102d Congress, 2d session, Feb. 27, 1992.

taxpayer funds (along with private funds) in companies that develop technologies defined as critical or advanced by federal law. The under secretary, or the "venture capital czar,"[11] would make cheap funds available to venture capitalists by purchasing nonvoting preferred securities (direct loans and loan guarantees). The czar would then regulate and investigate licensees as necessary to ensure compliance with the bill's provisions, such as the requirement that at least 50 percent of a licensed fund's investments be in "seed and early stage financing."[12] Unlike its predecessors, this proposal has made it out of committee, passing the full House and the Senate Commerce Committee.[13]

Gone are the days when industrial policy proposals died in committee or were listed as DOA at the White House. Instead, in a clear departure from the Bush line, President Clinton entered the White House arguing both the appropriateness and the necessity of direct government support for the "development, commercialization, and deployment of new technology." His presidency preaches a new faith in the ability of government to harness technology and change. In venture capital, the bet is that government can help lower the investment risk and spur venture capitalists onward toward creating the jobs and the high-tech, twenty-first-century economy that Clinton promised Americans during the campaign. In particular, his technology plan calls for special "incentives for those who make

---

[11]T. J. Rodgers, "Subsidies with Deathly Strings," *Forbes*, July 19, 1993, p. 206.

[12]H.R. 820, Title III, Sec. 347(d)(2), 103d Congress, 1st session, Feb. 4, 1993.

[13]The National Competitiveness Act of 1993 was passed by the House on May 19 and reported out of the Senate Commerce Committee on May 25, 1993.

high-risk, long-term venture capital investments in start-ups and other small enterprises."[14]

How these investors in the venture capital pool should be encouraged remains, however, a divisive issue—even among Democrats. President Clinton has focused on the tax option, resurrecting Senator Dale Bumpers's (D-Ark.) 1991 proposal to exclude from taxes half the capital gains on investments in new businesses held for more than five years.[15] The administration has also criticized House Democrats for jumping out ahead of the White House with their program to give the Commerce Department the responsibilities of a venture capitalist, which would be "counter-productive to the achievement of the [competitiveness] objectives of H.R. 820, and . . . may have unintended, serious consequences."[16]

Others less constrained by party politics have argued that the Department of Commerce is no place for a new investment program that is expected to make

---

[14]Office of the President, *Technology for America's Economic Growth* (Washington, D.C.: GPO, February 22, 1993), p. 12.

[15]Office of the President, *A Vision for Change for America* (Washington, D.C.: Government Printing Office, February 17, 1993), p. 62. The implementing legislation proposed by Senator Bumpers and Representative Robert T. Matsui (D-Calif.) passed the House but was dropped from the Senate version as part of a compromise deficit reduction package. At this writing, reconciliation of House and Senate packages had not yet taken place. See Senator Bumpers, S. 368 (The Enterprise Capital Formation Act of 1993), 103d Congress, 1st session, Feb. 16, 1993 and S. 1932, 102d Congress, 1st session, Nov. 7, 1991.

[16]Letter to Representative Robert S. Walker (R-Pa.), ranking minority member, Committee on Science, Space, and Technology, from General Counsel of U.S. Department of Commerce, April 21, 1993.

the venture capital market more efficient. Claude Barfield of the American Enterprise Institute has argued, for example, that "it is a lethal combination to have in one department the bureaucracy which not only subsidizes U.S. industry, but also is mandated to protect that industry. Inevitably those two policies will collide."[17]

Fortunately, this collision has been delayed—at least temporarily—by budget battles and the territorial dispute between the Small Business Administration and the Commerce Department over which one will play the lead role in helping young high-tech companies. The 1993 competitiveness package would make the Commerce Department the winner. But Bumpers, chairman of the Senate Small Business Committee, has vehemently protested that the new commerce program would come out of SBA's budget and duplicate an existing program. In his opening statement at a hearing on June 9, 1993, Bumpers said, "This new 'wannabe' program feeds from the same trough as existing small business programs . . . and I know we don't have enough seed corn to go around for existing programs."[18] One program in particular that Bumpers would like to continue to feed is the Small Business Investment Company (SBIC) program.

---

[17]House of Representatives, *National Competitiveness Act of 1993: Report together with Dissenting Views to Accompany H.R. 820*, 103d Congress, 1st session, May 3, 1993, H. Rept. 103-77, p. 53.

[18]Senate Committee on Small Business, *Investment in Critical Technologies through the Small Business Administration's Existing Financing Programs*, 103d Congress, 1st session, June 9, 1993, comments of Senator Dale Bumpers. See also, Jeanne Saddler, "SBA, Commerce Square Off on High Tech Financing," *Wall Street Journal*, June 9, 1993.

The program, created by Congress in 1958, is a federal government program for financing venture capitalists. The government has put almost $4 billion into the program, licensing and supporting privately owned and managed venture capital investment companies (SBICs).[19] According to the head of the SBA, "The SBA provides these licensed venture capitalists with financial assistance usually by guaranteeing their securities which are funded in the public markets. In some cases, the SBA purchases the licensee's securities directly."[20] The program helped firms like Nike and Cray Research get started but then lost over $600 million, after a rash of failures and the liquidations of more than 160 SBICs in the late 1980s.[21]

In 1992, the SBIC program was overhauled to shift the focus from debt to equity-based financing.[22] SBA's new administrator, Erskine Bowles, believes that as a result of the changes, "increased amounts of fi-

---

[19]Telephone interview with Maureen Glebes, staff economist, SBIC, Small Business Administration, August 24, 1993.

[20]U.S. Congress, Senate, Committee on Small Business, *Investment in Critical Technologies through the Small Business Administration's Existing Financing Programs,* 103d Congress, 1st session, June 9, 1993, written statement of Erskine B. Bowles, administrator of the Small Business Administration, pp. 2–3.

[21]Jeffry A. Timmons and William D. Bygrave, *Venture Capital at the Crossroads* (Boston: Harvard Business School Press, 1992), p. 28. U.S. Senate Small Business Committee, "Hearing to Receive the Holloway-Werner Report on SBA's Small Business Investment Company Program," 102d Congress, 1st session, July 16, 1991, p. 20.

[22]Before the 1992 overhaul, licensed venture capitalists (SBICs) had to make interest payments semiannually on the borrowed money, which made it difficult to make equity investments. Now SBICs will also be able to delay payment until they begin liquidating their investments in the companies.

nancing will flow to technology firms through the SBIC program beginning in FY94," and creating a program within SBA "to provide venture capital for critical technology will only enhance this activity."[23]

But the benefits would not be worth the cost, according to those pushing for the Commerce Department to become a high-tech "powerhouse." Senator Rockefeller has argued, for example, that SBA does not have the relevant experience to help early-stage high-tech companies because only 19 percent of past SBIC funding has gone to technology firms.[24]

Key Assumptions. Irrespective of how the turf and budget battles are ultimately resolved, congressional interest in financing entrepreneurs will no doubt continue.[25] The battles over policy direction provide, however, a unique opportunity for us to step back and evaluate whether anything is wrong with the market that needs to (or can) be fixed with a new or expanded federal program.

---

[23]Bowles, Senate Committee on Small Business, p. 9.

[24]Arguing that the high-tech experience of the SBA program had been misrepresented by its critics, Bowles testified that since 1958 SBICs have invested $1.6 billion in advanced technologies in their early years of development and during the past five years SBICs have provided an average of $100 million annually to technology-based firms. See Bowles, written testimony, p. 6.

[25]The Commerce Department venture capital program was scaled back from the proposed $100 million to $51 million for fiscal years 1994 and 1995 but with sharp increases planned for the subsequent years. In the first year, $1 million has been authorized for a feasibility study. The outcome of such a study has, however, apparently been predetermined given the $50 million already authorized to implement the program in FY1995.

Despite its long history, the Washington venture capital debate has focused more on form than on substance, that is, where a new program should be housed, who in government gets control, and how the program should be structured. Whether the market has fallen and "can't get up" without government assistance has, in contrast, received little attention. Missing in particular from the process are a serious economic study of and debate on four key assumptions.

• First, many assume that a capital gap faces would-be entrepreneurs and that that gap threatens U.S. competitiveness. Congressman George Brown (D-Calif.) and other advocates for a larger, direct government role believe that the gap exists because venture capital funds fell from a high of $4.2 billion in 1987 to less than $2 billion in 1991.[26] A particular concern is that the market is not investing enough in early-stage ventures because, according to some figures, professionally managed funds put less than 9 percent in start-ups in 1990—down from a peak of 43 percent in 1983.[27] This retreat has been held up in congressional debates as an ominous threat to America's job machine and to hopes for economic prosperity. Senator Rockefeller has raised, for example, the specter of foreigners moving in to fill the vacuum and thereby gaining control of America's innovative "seed corn."

---

[26]In a statement on the Senate floor by Senator Rockefeller, *Congressional Record,* 102d Congress, 2d session, Feb. 27, 1992, p. S2557.

[27]U.S. Congress, House of Representatives, Subcommittee on Technology, Environment and Aviation of the Committee on Science, Space, and Technology, *Hearing on the Technology Financing Provisions of H.R. 820, the National Competitiveness Act of 1993,* 103d Congress, 1st session, Feb. 16, 1993. Written testimony of Jeffry Timmons, p. 5.

• Second, many assume that more money for start-ups will generate more job growth. The future link between growth in the entrepreneurial segment of the economy and jobs may, however, have less to do with increasing the supply of early-stage capital and more to do with the regulations that influence how a company expands. Just as the decision to start a company hinges on many factors, the decision to add more jobs is also a multifaceted business decision. Fast-growing small companies add jobs when the price is right. Instead of holding down the price of an additional worker, federal policy in the form of new taxes and a growing regulatory burden (health, environment, and so forth) raises the price and thereby tends to dampen any job creation effect of start-ups and economic growth.

• Third, some believe that the government has a better idea than the market about the appropriate job of a professional venture capitalist. Underlying the proposals over the past four years is the conviction that there are not enough start-ups and that professionally managed funds therefore need to invest a larger share of their capital in the creation of new firms. Government is assumed to be as good as or better than private investors at knowing how much investment is enough and when prospective (social and private) returns justify more investment in start-ups.

• Hence, the fourth basic assumption: the government should boost the economy by using taxpayer funds either to induce the managers of venture capital funds to invest more in entrepreneurial firms or to purchase direct equity stakes for federal agencies in these firms.

To provide a foundation for exploring and debating these assumptions, the next two sections offer a brief overview of venture capital funds and the primary attributes of the American system of entrepreneurial finance.

Venture Capital Funds

Today when one speaks about venture capital, the now familiar names of Digital Equipment, Apple, Lotus, and Federal Express are often invoked to describe the catalytic role of those visionary risk-takers who helped to create these firms and thereby change the way America lives and works. Venture capital, although clearly not the only factor, was instrumental in developing semiconductors, personal computing, overnight delivery service, biotechnology, and other revolutionary industries.

In the beginning, the venture capital industry consisted of a handful of firms established by wealthy individuals to provide equity financing for young, entrepreneurial companies that did not yet have access to bank credit or to the public securities market. Although the first venture capital fund, American Research & Development, was started in 1946, the industry remained in an embryonic state for three decades. In the 1970s, the industry still consisted of a small number of firms managing modest pools of capital with little specialization or competition for deals. Then, in the early 1980s the industry surged forward, creating an energetic, frantic, and heterogeneous marketplace that soared from $4 billion to over $35 billion in the cumulative capital pool. Today, venture capital funds invest over $2 billion annually in roughly 2,000 entrepreneurial ventures (see figure 1–1).

The professional market is made up of managed funds that provide capital, management advice, and contacts to enterprises, ranging from seed level to mature companies.[28] The business of a venture capitalist is

---

[28]The life cycle of a new enterprise usually involves multiple stages of financing and growth. During the seed and start-up

13

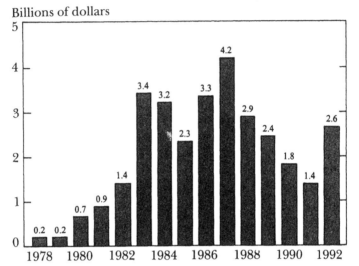

FIGURE 1-1
NEW CAPITAL COMMITTED PER YEAR
TO INDEPENDENT VENTURE CAPITAL FIRMS, 1978–1992

Billions of dollars

SOURCE: Venture Capital Yearbook 1992–93.

to find promising, privately held companies, grow them
into successful businesses, and then exit by selling the
companies to larger firms or taking them public. A ten-
year partnership has evolved as the dominant form for a
venture capital firm. The general partners manage the
fund, shoulder the legal responsibility, and typically contribute 1 percent of the capital. They raise the rest of

stages relatively small amounts of capital are typically needed to
transform an idea into a marketable product or service. In
stages 1 and 2, sales start to take off, and growth accelerates
with revenue between $2 million and $25 million. During stages
3 and 4, firms rely on public financing as they reach profitabil-
ity and a sustainable growth rate with revenues typically in the
$25 million or greater range. "Aspects of Performance in the
High Technology Sector," p. 32.

the capital base from partners such as pension funds, institutions, and wealthy individuals who are limited in their liabilities and management control. Venture capitalists keep on average 20 percent of the return and then distribute the rest to the limited partners.[29]

The industry grew out of the need in the postwar period to finance high-tech start-ups and to cover the substantial risks associated with breakthrough innovations. Banks and other traditional lending institutions were not set up to handle the risks of start-ups, which need financing up front but often do not offer any prospect of a payment for five to seven years versus the one to three years it may take a mature company to produce a product at a profit. With banks unable to wait, the market for venture capital emerged to fill the gap. In contrast to banks, venture capital firms are organized to operate with a low success rate as they actively seek out those companies that have the potential to change the world. Well-known success stories include Genetech, Compaq Computer, and Sun Microsystems, which were all launched with venture capital funds in the 1970s. Unlike banks, venture capital funds do not lend but take instead an ownership stake in companies.

Venture capital is often associated with "patient" capital, because, unlike debt financing, a firm using venture capital does not need to make interest or principal payments during the early years when cash-flow requirements are the greatest. The long-term nature of these investments is reflected in the analysis of distributions to paid-in capital by Venture Economics, which found that even those venture funds in the top tier are not making significant distributions until their fifth year of operation; the original committed capital is not

---

[29]Timmons and Bygrave, *Venture Capital at the Crossroads,* pp. 10–12.

typically returned until between the seventh and the eighth year of operation.[30]

As in most industries, the aging process in the venture capital market has brought fundamental change: institutions have replaced individuals as the primary investor in venture funds; megafunds (over $100 million) have come to dominate the fund-raising business; the average deal has increased to over $1 million; and the focus of venture funds in these deals has shifted from early-stage to expansion-stage financing.[31] Much of the policy debate concerns the shift of these funds away from so-called classic venture capitalism or small-dollar equity stakes in high-tech start-ups. On one side are those like the sponsors of the venture capital provision in H.R. 820. They argue that the shift has left many good *ideas* unfunded, creating a choke hold on the engine that gives America its competitive advantage in global markets. Critics counter with two points: there is no evidence that good *deals*—early stage or otherwise—are being ignored by investors; and the economic and policy importance of the shift has been exaggerated be-

[30] *1992 Investment Benchmark Report: Venture Capital,* Venture Economics, pp. 7–8.

[31] According to Venture Economics, the pension fund share has grown from 15 percent in 1978 to 42 percent of new capital commitments in 1992, a year in which all institutional investors supplied 89 percent of the new capital commitments to venture funds. In the 1990–1991 period, megafunds captured two-thirds of the total capital commitment to venture funds. The megafund cost structure favors larger investments because of efficiency gains from dividing funds into segments of $2 million as opposed to many $250,000 lumps. Ted R. Dintersmith, "Challenges, Opportunities in Early-Stage," *Venture Capital Journal,* January 1993, pp. 4, 34. See also, Bruce Posner, "How to Finance Anything," *Inc.,* February 1993, pp. 54–68.

cause venture capital funds are not the most important source of capital for entrepreneurs.

President Clinton has promised to use government as a tool to ensure that "change becomes our friend rather than our enemy." In venture capital, this begs the question whether change without government direction or administrative guidance has been detrimental to the health of the entrepreneurial community. To make sense of the debate, it helps to consider first the attributes of the industry that influence the nature of the government's role.

Industry Characteristics

Five features of venture capital and the entrepreneurial finance system stand out as particularly relevant for any discussion of the role of government. Together, they point to the critical role of prospective returns in understanding the performance of the U.S. market. These returns will in turn depend on risk, the availability of good ideas and sound management teams, competition and other market conditions in venture capital, and the general health of the U.S. financial markets.

High-Risk Ballgame. Venture capital is first and foremost a business of high risks and high prospective returns. As one might expect, attempts to discover and develop tomorrow's Fortune 500 companies frequently fail. To offset the risk, the goal on each project is often supernormal profits—sometimes twice the average return on bonds and other more liquid investments. Everyone is looking for a home run or the next Apple Computer, which in seven years reached over $500 million in sales and opened up the personal computer market by challenging the status quo, that is, IBM. Or, as Benno Schmidt, Sr.,

17

managing partner of the New York venture capital firm J.H. Whitney & Company, put it, "We don't live so much on our batting average as on our slugging average."[32]

The trick is finding and growing those companies with the potential to shake up an industry. The investment risk is extraordinary. Even without the home run aspirations, the time it takes to build a company and to realize an adequate gain generates terrible odds, especially in fast-moving high-tech sectors. One venture capitalist, Frank Bonsal, compared the risk to that of horse breeding and racing: only one-third of new companies succeed, and only one in a hundred is a big winner. In particular, Venture Economics, the leading market research firm, found in a survey of venture capital portfolios that of the 383 investments made by thirteen funds between 1969 and 1985, one-third resulted in a partial or total loss, while less than 7 percent of the capital invested resulted in payoffs of more than ten to one.[33]

More than Good Ideas. To accept the risk, venture capitalists require not only supernormal returns but also an influential voice in the management of the company.

Management matters because the business of venture capital demands much more than good ideas. As we move beyond anecdotes to the pattern of successful start-ups, as a recent *Inc.* market study did, we find that startups do not succeed by accident or for the reasons often paraded before congressional committees. More than a lot of money, more than the will of the founder, and

---

[32]Liz Roman Gallese, "Venture Capital Strays Far from Its Roots," *New York Times,* April 1, 1990.

[33]Venture Economics, "Venture Capital Performance: Review of the Financial Performance of Venture Capital Partnerships," Venture Economics, Inc., 1988; Bill Sahlman,"Insights from the American Venture Capital Organization," p. 47.

more than even the product itself, spectacular sales and job growth depend on the people involved and how they put the company together.[34] As William Sahlman of Harvard Business School points out, without sound management, a good idea will remain just that—an idea, instead of a successful product line and company. Apple succeeded not only because it had a good idea and good luck but also because management advice from such business heavyweights as Arthur Rock, Teledyne chairman Henry Singleton, Mike Markkula, and Regis McKenna helped put together Apple's winning business plan and marketing strategy.[35] Indeed, Mr. Rock has said that nearly every mistake he has made "has been in picking the wrong people, not the wrong idea." "Most entrepreneurs," he says, "have no problem coming up with a good strategy, but they usually need all the help they can get in developing and implementing the tactics that will make them successful in the long run."[36]

On the fund-raising side of the business, experienced managers have become an increasingly important factor. Or, as John Doerr, a San Francisco venture capitalist put it, "The biggest shortage is the people with the know-how, not the capital."[37] The enormous influx of capital into the industry over a decade ago brought with it a rush of new and inexperienced managers who often financed marginal companies at high valuations. Many ran into problems and recorded tremendous losses—

---

[34]For results of the study taken from the *Inc.* database, see Leslie Brokaw, "The Truth about Start-ups," *Inc.*, March 1993, pp. 56–64.

[35]Michael Orme, "Apple's New Ball-Game," *Management Today,* August 1983, pp. 62–65.

[36]As quoted by Timmons and Bygrave, *Venture Capital at the Crossroads,* p. 6.

[37]Ibid., quoting speech given at 1990 Venture Forum, p. 29.

proving that more venture capital is not always better.[38] In the 1990s, the premium the market puts on experience shows up in the data on capital under management: over 60 percent of funds raised in 1992 went into firms whose partners had ten or more years of experience.[39]

Subject to Ups and Downs. But experience is not everything. Perhaps more important to understanding the industry and its problems is an appreciation for the cyclical nature of venture capital, which shadows the movement of the broader economy. The economic environment in which funds are invested will significantly affect results. High returns for venture funds were, for example, achieved in the 1976–1980 period in large part because of a good investing and exiting environment. In contrast, the funds started in 1982 invested during a time of intense competition and high valuations and typically generated low returns.

Consider, for example, the late 1970s, which marked the beginning of a venture capital cycle. Rapid technological change provided start-ups a range of opportunities to exploit such as personal computers and new discoveries such as gene splicing. The prospect of supernormal profits and a booming stock market generated a gold rush, drawing in record numbers of investors and triggering an explosion in new capital commitments: during 1982–1987, new commitments increased

---

[38]The wide deviation of significant returns for funds started in the 1980s reflects, for example, the significant range of experience and ability. For those started in 1983, returns ranged from –14.4 percent to 25.5 percent. *1992 Investment Benchmarks Report*, p. 6.

[39]Michael Vachon, "Venture Capital Reborn," *Venture Capital Journal*, January 1993, p. 34.

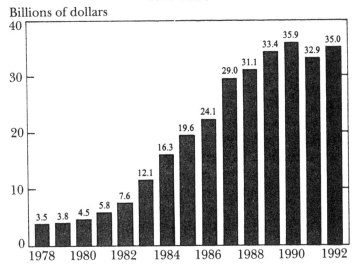

FIGURE 1–2
Total Capital under Management, 1978–1992

Billions of dollars

SOURCE: Venture Capital Yearbook 1992–93.

at an unsustainable rate of 30 percent a year as the cumulative market pool soared upward (see figure 1–2).

The surging market soon became a victim of its own success, as market overcrowding became a serious problem and venture capital became a seller's market. During 1978–1988, the number of professional venture capital firms increased from 230 to more than 650—all fighting for a share of the deal pool. For each good idea—disk drives, laptops, or printers—twelve or thirteen companies were started. In the case of disk drives, more than forty start-ups were financed. Start-up companies initially took on the big companies such as IBM, but then they began to compete with one another— sometimes in the same venture capital fund portfolio, straining management and technology resources.

The 1987 stock market crash also helped to deflate the market.[40] The burst of start-up activity in the 1982–1985 period had produced a full pipeline of growing companies ready and registered to go public. But then the public market for new securities dried up in the wake of the crash, making it difficult for venture capitalists to cash out and turn in acceptable returns on investment.

In response, returns fell after 1983, and the market plummeted.[41] According to Venture Economics, funds started between 1976 and 1979 generated an average internal rate of return of 27.3 percent. By contrast, the return for those formed during 1981–1987 ranged from 2.2 to 7.5 percent.[42]

The poor exit market and lackluster return performance discouraged investment in venture funds, helping to push the market downward almost as dramatically as the upswing six to seven years earlier. The

---

[40]The 1986 increase in the top capital gains rate from 20 to 33 percent is another factor some analysts credit with causing the decline in venture capital.

[41]Regarding the correlation between investment returns and market activity, returns have been strongest in the years in which industry both raised and invested less than $2 billion. Returns started to decline when venture capital fund raising and investments consistently topped $2.5 billion during the 1983–1987 period.

[42]Averages in venture capital are not, however, the best indicator of potential return, because over the past decade the venture capital industry has split into two tiers marked by a wide deviation among returns for any given year. For a better indicator of the decline in returns, consider the top tier, or first quartile, funds that generated a return of 40.3 percent for funds started in 1976–1979 versus 14.3 to 6.8 percent for 1981–1987 funds. *1992 Investment Benchmarks Report*, pp. 6, 7.

market fell from its peak flow of $4 billion in new capital in 1987 to $1.4 billion in 1991, and disbursements to entrepreneurial firms fell on average 25 percent a year (see figure 1-1).

To understand the drop, consider the expectations of investors who invested when the market was rising in the early 1980s versus those who invested in 1988. From the five-year performance record of venture capital funds, 1988 investors would have seen that actual returns were off and that invested capital was taking longer than expected to payoff. Funds started in 1982, for example, had returned only 25 percent of "paid in" value by 1987 in contrast to the four to five years it took funds started in the late 1970s to return the original committed capital (see table 1-1).[43]

The market picked itself up again after a four-year slide. Prospective returns increased, and in 1992, venture capital funds raised $2.6 billion, nearly double the 1991 level. Flush with cash, venture capitalists are investing in a new range of technologies such as biopharmaceuticals.[44] A renewed sense of excitement pervades the market as investors analyze what many consider to be the most attractive environment for deals in the past ten to twelve years: opportunities are up, the number of active venture capital firms is down to around 200, and valuations in the public market are more reasonable. Even enthusiasm among institutional investors is up again. The Klynveld Peat Marwick Goerdeler (KPMG) 1993 survey of institutional investors found that for the first time in three years venture cap-

---

[43]Ibid., pp. 7–8.
[44]"The Time Is Ripe for Seed and Early-Stage," *Venture Capital Journal,* December 12, 1992, p. 13.

TABLE 1-1
DISTRIBUTION TO PAID-IN CAPITAL, 1976–1982

	Year Fund Started			
After "X" Years	1976–79	1980	1981	1982
1	0.00	0.01	0.00	0.00
2	0.04	0.08	0.04	0.02
3	0.32	0.33	0.08	0.05
4	0.92	0.50	0.14	0.13
5	1.70	0.74	0.40	0.25
6		1.00	0.70	0.36
7			0.90	0.51
8			1.02	0.67

NOTE: A value of 1 indicates original capital returned.
SOURCE: Venture Economics, *1992 Investment Benchmarks,* p. 7.

ital swept all other asset classes with an expected ten-year return of 13.4 percent.[45]

The rebound in the venture capital market was spurred in part by the upswing in U.S. equity markets and in part by a newly resurgent initial public offering (IPO) market. A vibrant IPO market gives investors a stronger incentive to invest because of the improved opportunity to liquidate portfolio companies. In 1991, the IPO market reached a record level of 121 venture-backed firms going public—more than in the 1988–1990 period combined and the most since the last good IPO market in 1983 (see figure 1-3). The IPO market continued upward in 1992 with 151 ven-

---

[45]Falling interest rates and the consequent blow to future fixed-income returns are encouraging institutional investors to revisit venture capital to compensate for low yields. Kathleen Devlin, "Post-Venture Dilemma," ibid., May 1993, p. 32.

FIGURE 1–3

INITIAL PUBLIC OFFERINGS OF
PRIVATE, VENTURE-CAPITAL–BACKED ENTERPRISES, 1981–1992

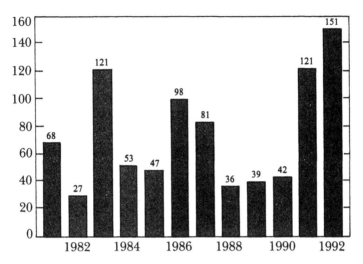

SOURCES: Venture Capital Yearbook 1992–93, Venture Capital Journal, February, 1993.

ture-backed companies going public out of a total of 595 companies.[46]

Interest in start-ups and early-stage companies is on the upswing once again. In the 1980s, leveraged buyouts (LBOs) were popular. But the collapse of the junk bond market in 1989 cooled the attraction. In 1989, venture capital investment in LBOs fell by 31 percent, while seed financing increased. Then in 1991, venture capital invested in LBOs fell by an additional 87 percent to $45.8 million, down nearly $1 billion from the high of $1.1 billion in 1988.[47] Meanwhile,

---

[46]Vachon, "Venture Capital Reborn," p. 35.

[47]Kathleen Devlin, "Disbursements Hit 10-Year Low," *Venture Capital Journal,* June 1992, p. 29.

seed investing soared from $76 million in 1991 to $209 million in 1992.

The trend is expected to continue as investors shift away from later-stage investments where profits have been shrinking.[48] Indeed, many argue that basic economics and the cyclical nature of the industry are sparking a comeback of funds for seed financing. Seed financing is "coming back into vogue," according to William Wetzel, Forbes Professor of Management at the University of New Hampshire. With low prices and high quality investment opportunities, the lure of attractive deals may be too great for investors to stay away. One survey of seed and start-up funds, for example, Emory's 1991 census, found a 19 percent average return on investment—well above the industry norm.[49]

Much More than Professional Funds. Over the past two decades, a vibrant and diverse market has evolved in the United States for financing new enterprises. In addition to the professionally managed venture capital funds, the sources of capital include internal funds (boot-strapping), private individuals (business angels), and corporations. The informal nature of these other

---

[48]Udayan Gupta, "Venture Capital Investment Soars, Reversing 4-Year Slide," *Wall Street Journal,* June 1, 1993. For recovery of start-up financing, see also David T. Gleba, "Venture Funding Recovery?" *Upside,* July 1993, p. 65.

[49]Caution must, however, be exercised in extending Emory's census results because of the small number of funds (fourteen) on which actual returns are based. The included funds may also be of different vintage years. Emory Business School, *1991 National Census of Public and Private Seed Capital Funds,* sponsored by KPMG Peat Marwick, Emory Business School, 1991, p. 20. See also Kathleen Devlin, "Seed Stage Rebirth," *Venture Capital Journal,* July 1992, p. 32.

sources of capital precludes a comprehensive database either to track with precision the aggregate pool of capital or to break down in detail the relative importance of the different funding sources. Most of the information available is based on the organized professional fund component of the market, perhaps explaining—but not justifying—the near complete focus of congressional hearings and the previous policy discussions on these funds as a proxy for the health of the entrepreneurial community.

The popular notion in Washington that most new high-tech companies are funded by venture capitalists is, for example, highly misleading. Instead, the available evidence, market analysis, and industry information suggest that these funds—the business that activists in Washington have been trying to boost—play a small and declining role in the formation of new businesses. The Small Business Administration estimates that 600,000 to 700,000 firms are created each year, with less than 1 percent (or 1,000 to 2,000 firms) financed by professional venture capitalists. Among high-tech enterprises, the venture fund share is somewhat higher but still less than 20 percent.[50] As Paul Reynolds of the Center for the Study of Entrepreneurship in Milwaukee put it, "That's the way the world is; the venture capitalists are on the periphery of the real action."[51]

Therefore, to avoid repeating the mistake of searching for answers only where the proverbial street light happens to shine, any serious discussion of the "capital gap" needs to recognize the diverse and sometimes complementary sources of entrepreneurial fi-

[50]William Whiston and Charles Ou, Small Business Administration, telephone interviews with author on April 6, 1993.
[51]Brokaw, "The Truth About Start-ups," p. 64.

nancing. Even with the recent upturn in the venture capital market, few industry analysts expect professional venture capitalists to supplant angels and corporations as the primary providers of equity financing.[52]

Business angels are the commercial equivalent of Broadway angels in the world of theater. They are typically retired executives and self-made individuals with a high net worth who have built companies themselves, such as Ross Perot (EDS), Mitch Kapor (Lotus), and Alex D'Arberloff (Teradyne). Over the past decade, these individuals have grown in number and reputation as an attractive source of equity. By almost any available measure, the capital contributions they make dwarf those of venture capitalists. A White House report, *Aspects of Performance in the High Technology Sector,* found that over the 1985–1988 period, the annual flow of equity capital from informal investors was roughly $32.7 billion versus the $3.2 billion average annual flow from venture capitalists.[53] Angels also complement the financing role of venture capitalists. Relative

---

[52]Udayan Gupta, "Venture Capital Dims for Start-ups, but Not to Worry," *Wall Street Journal,* Jan. 24, 1990, p. B2.

[53]Executive Office of the President, Office of Science and Technology Policy, "Aspects of Performance in the High Technology Sector," Issues in Science and Technology Policy Working Paper, January 7, 1993, p. 35; *Venture Capital Yearbook 1992,* Venture Economics, p. 23; and Robert J. Gaston and Sharon E. Bell, *The Informal Supply of Capital,* Applied Economics Group, Inc. for U.S. Small Business Administration, Office of Economic Research, September 1988. See also William Wetzel, director of the Center for Venture Research at the University of New Hampshire, who estimates that there are about 250,000 business angels who invest in 30,000 new ventures each year. Memorandum "Presidential Transition Roundtable Meeting," Center for Venture Research, University of New Hampshire, December 2, 1992.

to professional venture capitalists, they tend to invest smaller amounts (less than $50,000) at earlier stages, accounting for over 48 percent of seed investment in small, high-tech firms. Almost 60 percent of informal investments are in early-stage ventures versus the 10–15 percent share in venture capital funds.[54]

Internal or boot-strap financing also plays an invaluable, although often overlooked, role in the early stages. One of the best known boot-strappers is Ross Perot, who took $1,000 and turned it into the multibillion dollar EDS Corporation. Although boot-strappers rarely turn into presidential candidates, Perot may be more the rule than the exception in the world of entrepreneurial finance. A detailed study of U.S. start-ups found, for example, that high-growth companies rely more on their own boot straps than on professional venture capitalists. The study done by Amar Bhide of Harvard Business School surveyed 100 of the fastest-growing companies started between 1982 and 1989 and found that 75 percent were principally self-financed (personal savings, credit cards, and second mortgages), whereas in 1990 only 5 percent were backed by venture capital.[55] For the critical start-up capital stage, the 1992 *Inc.* survey found that 79 per-

---

[54]Over the past decade, the average deal for venture capitalists has increased to over $1 million, while almost two-thirds of angel investments remain less than $50,000. See Executive Office of the President, "Aspects of Performance in the High Technology Sector," pp. 35–36. Also Devlin, "Disbursements Hit 10-Year Low," p. 29. Alex Alger, "Venture Capital Disbursements Rise," *Venture Capital Journal,* June 1993, p. 33.

[55]For results of survey, see Amar Bhide, "Bootstrap Finance: The Art of Start-ups," *Harvard Business Review* (November–December, 1992). See also, Timmons and Bygrave, *Venture Capital at the Crossroads,* p. 34.

cent of the fastest-growing companies relied on personal savings, while only 6.3 percent were supplied by
formal venture capital funds.[56] In software—a critical
industry in which the United States leads the world—a
nationwide survey of over 700 companies conducted
by Price Waterhouse and the Massachusetts Computer
Software Council found that 80 percent have been self-
financed.[57]

With these results, Amar Bhide and other analysts
have made the case that venture capital funds are no
longer the appropriate model for meeting the needs of
most new firms. Bhide suggests sound financial reasons
for the shift of these funds away from start-ups: before
the venture capital business surged and matured in the
1980s, it may have made sense for fund managers to
focus more on start-ups, but given the significant costs
incurred in investigating and monitoring investments,
these managers have developed exacting criteria that
most start-ups cannot meet. These include large-scale,
proprietary advantages, well-defined plans, founders
with solid reputations, and "home run" potential. Nor
should start-ups expend valuable time and brain power
trying to meet these standards. According to Bhide
and other market analysts, change has been good: venture capital funds were the wrong place to look even in
the best of times given the small-scale nature of financing most start-ups and the hidden costs (premature
funding, loss of flexibility and control) of working with
venture capital funds.[58]

---

[56]Martha E. Mangelsdorf, "Behind the Scenes," *Inc.*, October
1992, p. 80.
[57]Price Waterhouse, *1992 Software Industry Business Practices Survey* (Massachusetts Computer Software Council, Inc. and Price
Waterhouse, 1992).
[58]In addition to Bhide, see Bruce G. Posner, "How to Finance Any-

As an alternative, corporations provide an increasingly important source of capital for entrepreneurs. If the downsizing trend continues as expected in corporate America, executives will continue to search out new ways to trim costs and improve efficiency. From this perspective, entrepreneurial companies are an attractive, strategic proposition. Economies of scale in marketing and distribution combined with the creative energy of these firms make a strong case for a deal. Entrepreneurs get financial stability and are freed from the day-to-day headaches of running a company, while the larger firm can improve its customer base and gain exposure to new product ideas. Two-thirds of those software companies in the Price Waterhouse survey, for example, listed larger firms as a capital source through partnerships or alliances.[59]

The Envy of the World. The American capital market for entrepreneurs has become the model for major industrial countries. Start-ups outside the United States often face a daunting challenge of hostile corporate cultures, stifling regulations, and a powerful alliance between large, established firms and the political elite.

In Japan, for example, would-be entrepreneurs face investors who do not want to take risks on start-ups and a business culture that scorns smallness and the free-wheeling spirit. Rather than prizing individual entrepreneurs who challenge the status quo, Japan val-

---

thing," *Inc.*, February 1993, pp. 54–68. Also, William Wetzel, who has argued that "even in the best of financial times, venture capital funds are not the place to look for early-stage financing. Entrepreneurs have been knocking on the wrong doors in their search for funds." "The Truth about Angels More than a Myth," Center for Venture Research, University of New Hampshire, Winter 1993.

[59] *The Economist*, September 21, 1991, p. 90.

ues established reputations and stable growth. Top graduates become bureaucrats or go to large companies, reinforcing a culture that has been described as "venture capital's greatest enemy."[60] The lingering effect of regulations, which limited until the late 1980s the listing of small company stock, still keeps the initial public offerings in Tokyo to less than one-third of Nasdaq. The result is few start-ups. Even during the downturn in the American venture capital market, the number of new firms formed in the United States was ten times as great as in Japan. The cumulative venture capital pool in Japan of $6.6 billion also contrasted with the $33 billion managed by American professional funds in 1991.[61] In Europe, the culture is somewhat less hostile to start-ups, but the market is still small, static, and underdeveloped in comparison with that of the United States.

What's the Problem?

To draw out the policy implications from the data and trends in entrepreneurial finance, this volume explores the proposition that the venture capital market needs a direct boost from government. The contributors draw on their own research and the insights of other key members of the policy, research, and business communities.

The authors first consider whether the balance of evidence suggests that the United States is underinvesting in "good ideas" or start-ups. They split over whether

[60]Stephen Yoder, "Japanese Venture Capitalist Preaches American Sermon," *Wall Street Journal,* July 3, 1989.
[61]"Venture Capital Becomes a Scarce Resource," *Financial Times,* September 30, 1992, and "Japan Caution Prevails," *Financial Times,* September 21, 1993.

the downturn in venture capital and start-up financing in the late 1980s could be explained by self-correcting, cyclical movements.

On the side of a structural capital deficit, Anthony Clark argues that far from being healthy, the United States suffers from chronic underinvestment in risky enterprises. He traces the problem to the shift toward institutions as the primary supplier of capital to venture funds, which he believes creates structural barriers to early-stage financing. According to Mr. Clark, "About 90 percent of professional venture capital now comes from institutions that demand liquidity and short payback periods. As a result, the size of funds has increased, the dollar value of the average deal has increased, and there has been a shift toward later-stage transactions." Mr. Clark stresses that the short payback time frame of institutional investors conflicts with the time-consuming, small-scale, long-term nature of early-stage investing. Mr. Clark concludes that the gap in start-up financing will not be closed by a cyclical upturn in the market. Instead, fund managers, driven by the demands of their institutional partners, will continue to look for larger, shorter-term investments.

William Sahlman does not share Mr. Clark's concern about the shift toward institutional investors, arguing that "to imagine that the United States is suffering from a shortage of capital going into high-growth or high-potential ventures is simply wrong." Instead of an allocation problem or a capital gap, Sahlman's research finds "little evidence that ventures that should get funded are denied access to capital, even when new capital commitments to the professional venture capital industry decline."[62]

---

[62]William Sahlman, "Insights from the American Venture Capi-

On the presumed deficit in early-stage ventures, Sahlman refers to his "field of dreams theory." "If there is a shortage," he says, "investors will come. If there are high prospective rates of return, I have great faith that my colleagues in the investment community will figure it out, move to capture those returns, and the market will correct itself." Sahlman and Florida further argue that, because many more start-ups are funded outside the professional market by individuals and corporations, the policy focus on the professional venture capital funds exaggerates the importance of the structural changes and misses the big picture, which is healthy. The Council on Competitiveness found in a recent report, for example, that the United States does well in high-risk, long time horizon start-ups and invests heavily in such emerging industries as cellular communications and biotechnology.[63]

Rather than "growing deficiencies in the domestic venture capital market," Sahlman finds that the comparative strength of the dynamic American market is increasing. In Europe, venture capital is more of an idea than a flourishing market, while Sahlman has found the corporate community in Japan to be particu-

---

tal Organization," working paper for the Council on Competitiveness and the Harvard Business School Project on Corporate Investment, March 1992, p. 34. In addition, according to Ian Ross, NAC's chairman, "There's venture capital in considerable quantity out there. The problem is that it's too high priced." Ross then argued that cost of venture capital will come down when Americans begin saving more and the federal budget is balanced. See Graeme Browning, "Targeting High Tech," *National Journal*, January 11, 1992, p. 72.

[63]Michael Porter, *Capital Choices: Changing the Way America Invests in Industry*, Council on Competitiveness and the Harvard Business School, June 1992, p. 27.

larly hostile to funding start-ups. In contrast to these structural and cultural barriers, he concludes that the so-called problems in the American venture capital market are cyclical in nature: just as the market went down when returns fell, he sees the market turning upward as prospective rates of return climb. The downturn in commitments is itself not an indicator of a market failure.

Agreeing with Sahlman, Florida believes that what matters is not whether venture capital commitments are up or down but rather what is the efficient allocation of capital. Florida attacks the assumption behind much of the policy debate that the United States needs as much venture capital today as it had in the mid-1980s. He argues that the problem is not a shortage of venture capital now but rather that "the United States may have had too much venture capital then . . . with too many dollars chasing too few good ideas."

But like Clark, Florida believes that a cyclical upturn will not resolve some important structural competitiveness problems. Florida argues, however, that these problems are not in the venture capital market. He further points out that the "home run" orientation of the venture capital system biases investment in the direction of breakthrough innovations and new markets, crowding out investments in follow through, such as product refinement and improvements in manufacturing processes.[64] Given the competitiveness concern with commercial follow through and the structural bias of the venture capital system, Florida concludes that boosting venture capital, "while it may lead to more start-ups, may in fact be detrimental for the national economy."

[64]See also Richard Florida and Martin Kenney, *Breakthrough Illusion: Corporate America's Failure to Move from Innovation to Mass Production* (New York: Basic Books, 1990).

Is Underinvestment in Critical Technologies a Problem? Permeating almost all conversations on technology policy in Washington these days is the concern that the United States has failed to invest in those "critical" technologies that will boost long-term economic growth.[65] The authors of this book are no exception. If the social return to investment in these technologies exceeds the private return and the problem is prevalent, the argument goes, then perhaps the government should bridge the investment gap, at least for these technologies.

According to Anthony Clark, for example, the prevailing climate of risk aversion in the capital markets and venture capital in particular is impeding technology-based investments. In principle, William Sahlman agrees with Clark, but he questions how prevalent the market failures are in practice. Investment in high-tech areas such as software is, for example, on the upswing. In 1992, venture capitalists invested more in software and technology service businesses than any other area, investing over $550 million in 214 companies—a 63 percent increase from $337 million in 1991.[66]

---

[65]At last count, there were at least eleven or more critical technology reports circulating in Washington. See, for example, *Report of the National Critical Technologies Panel*, U.S. National Critical Technologies Panel, White House Office of Science and Technology Policy, Government Printing Office, 1991; Council on Competitiveness, *Gaining New Ground: Technology Priorities for America's Future*, Washington, D.C., 1991; Mary Ellen Mogee, "Technology Policy and Critical Technologies," discussion paper no. 3 (Manufacturing Forum, the National Academy of Engineering, December 1991).

[66]Alex Alger, "Venture Capital Disbursements Rise," p. 32.

Given the complex and dynamic nature of entrepreneurial finance, however, Sahlman is more concerned with the growing movement in Washington to favor one sector or set of technologies over another than with the swings of a particular industry. Critical industry lists and government programs could, for example, encourage too many investments in the same emerging industries and thereby unintentionally precipitate a market downturn similar to the one in the 1980s. If too much venture capital was a good thing, then perhaps we have no cause for concern. But both Florida and Sahlman argue that excessive investment, whether in start-ups, critical technologies, or venture capital, will divert resources from other productive uses and could therefore be as detrimental to economic growth as underinvestment. What matters is getting the balance right.

What Is the Government's Role?

In the interest of getting the investment balance right, the authors assessed how well equipped the government is to work with industry to determine the efficient level and distribution of risk capital across technologies and stages of development.

Too often, the debate over the proper government role in venture capital is reduced to picking winning ideas over losers. But venture capitalists do much more than just select good ideas. To be successful at managing a portfolio of firms, a venture capitalist must have the experience, knowledge, and flexibility to cut off support or determine how much additional support should be given. Professional investors are accustomed to a free-wheeling style and the freedom to select only those business plans that offer a reasonable

37

opportunity for a superior rate of return. They know from experience that not every "good idea" should be funded, especially if a good management team is missing. They also know that they will often have to make harsh decisions and shut off a large number of losers to profit from the winners and to generate adequate returns for their limited partners.

The Politics of Venture Capital. Do the Commerce Department and the SBA have the necessary management skills to fit into this high-risk business? Are congressional oversight committees and program administrators prepared to accept a one-in-ten success rate and the judgment of professionals on how public and private money should be allocated? Allan Meltzer of the American Enterprise Institute and Carnegie Mellon University has noted, for example, that governments find it hard "to close down firms that are not doing well" and easy "to pump in additional money to try to cover mistakes or misjudgments." He says "such money-losing tendencies are reinforced by congressional representatives, mayors, and local constituents that lobby to keep losers open, hoping for a better future." He points to the thrift industry debacle as an example of "what happens under such pressure."[67]

The tendency to impose noneconomic criteria on even well-meaning economic initiatives is already evident. In the debate over the venture capital program in H.R. 820, Senator Rockefeller has argued, for example, that the program would be particularly important for his state, West Virginia, and for "other states with active technology companies that are often overlooked

---

[67]Allan Meltzer, "Why Governments Make Bad Venture Capitalists," *Wall Street Journal,* May 5, 1993.

by the conventional venture capital markets."[68] In particular, the legislation calls for the licensed venture funds to engage in "outreach to economically depressed areas."[69]

But why has the market "overlooked" states like West Virginia? Market research by Richard Florida suggests that it is *not* because of a failure in the venture capital market. Instead, the evidence suggests that the market works: capital flows unimpeded by geography to those areas that offer the highest rates of return. Regions like Silicon Valley, New York City, and Route 128 around Boston have attracted capital because they have the supporting infrastructure (inputs and human resources) necessary to sustain high-technology entrepreneurship. As a result, Florida concludes that the "public provision of venture or risk capital is likely to be effective in only a very limited number of areas."[70]

If regional economic development is the policy objective, Florida concludes that venture capital is not the most effective tool: it is neither a problem nor a cure but rather a part of the broader challenge to boost competitiveness through greater technological capability. Likewise, if improving the efficiency of capital flows is the policy concern, then federal mandates like the one in H.R. 820 on regional distributions should be dropped because they are not supported by the economic evidence.

---

[68]Jay Rockefeller, *Congressional Record,* 103d Congress, 1st session, January 21, 1993, S256.

[69]H.R. 820, Title III, Subtitle D, Sec. 343(e), p. 69, 103d Congress, 1st session, as reported on May 3, 1993.

[70]Richard Florida and Martin Kenney, "Venture Capital and Economic Development," report to the U.S. Department of Commerce, Economic Development Administration, June 1990.

Oversight provisions on mandates like regional outreach have also traditionally provided another opportunity for mixing business and politics. The spectra of congressional micromanagement triggered protests even from proponents of a federal venture capital fund. In congressional testimony, for example, Jeffry Timmons of the Harvard Business School predicted that unless many of the oversight strings were cut, the standard practice of a venture capitalist to dismiss or demote a portfolio company's president would prompt phone calls from irritated constituents, political pressure to reverse the decision, and, ultimately, "mayhem."[71] Or, as T. J. Rodgers, president of Cypress Semiconductor, has argued, government involvement in venture capital would work to constrain, rather than to encourage, such disruptive surprises as Apple or any other innovators who threaten a politically connected employer or interest group.[72]

Political versus Economic Problems. Are the political problems more important than the suspected economic problems a federal venture capital program would try to redress?

On the side of intervention, Anthony Clark expresses the pending-crisis argument: if the government does not experiment and instead ignores the capital gap in start-up financing, the American innovative en-

---

[71]U.S. Congress, House of Representatives, Subcommittee on Technology, Environment, and Aviation of the Committee on Science, Space, and Technology, *Hearing on Technology Financing Provisions of H.R. 820, the National Competitiveness Act of 1993*, 103d Congress, 1st session, February 16, 1993, p. 9 of written testimony.
[72]Rogers, "Subsidies with Deathly Strings," p. 206.

gine that drives economic growth will be significantly impaired. Using the devastating Johnstown flood of 1880 as a lesson about the consequences of benign neglect and short-term thinking, Clark holds that the government should look beyond cyclical improvements to take the long-term perspective on financial markets. In particular, without some federal venture capital program to lower the risk in start-up financing, Clark concludes that the United States will make fewer attempts at revolutionary innovation and ultimately have a lower rate of technological progress and economic growth. He advocates a partnership that coinvests public and private funds, an arrangement he believes has an established record of success.

William Sahlman disagrees with Clark, arguing that any so-called market failures are unlikely to be relieved through greater government intervention. Instead, given the dramatic failures of the SBIC program and the dynamic nature of entrepreneurial finance, Sahlman predicts that the unintended costs of a venture capital program would likely swamp any benefits of the program. An an example of how well-intentioned federal targeting is already missing the mark, Sahlman points to the current policy focus on professional venture capitalists. If early-stage financing for would-be entrepreneurs is the driving concern, as suggested by Clark and the various sponsors of federal venture capital initiatives, then Sahlman argues that a more appropriate effort would be to strengthen the investment incentives of private individuals and boot-strappers who together provide most of this type of financing.

Sahlman also attacks the popular assumption that government policy, whether through capital gains taxes or subsidies, will have a direct effect on the start-up rate. Evidence in favor of the proposition he finds to be slim at best, because in the real world the decision to start a business turns on many other factors. After the home run has been hit or the business has taken off, then perhaps changes in the capital gains rate will play a bigger role in such decisions as how fast to grow the company.

Given the government's troubled track record in venture capital, Richard Florida also wondered why Congress would want to do more. In particular, Dr. Florida suggests that the SBIC program may have outlived its usefulness given its recent problems and the dramatic growth of the private market over the past two decades—especially the emergence of the venture capital limited partnership.

He believes these problems are best left to business and local governments to correct, while the federal government should concentrate on taking apart, rather than adding to, the layer cake of regulations and new programs that impede economic growth. For starters, he suggests that Washington learn from the costly mistakes made by states when they moved to fill the venture "capital gap": they misdiagnosed the problem and used the wrong tools to boost economic development. As a result, the states failed to increase entrepreneurial activity with public funds, and they are now abandoning their venture capital programs.[73]

Areas for Further Study

As is often the case, more questions have been raised than could be adequately addressed. Three questions stand out as particularly relevant to the issue of entrepreneurial finance and government policy.

---

[73]Florida and Kenney, "Venture Capital and Economic Development."

- To what extent will small, high-tech firms be future job machines for the economy?[74]
- To what extent do social returns from start-up activity differ from private returns?
- What evidence is there that the United States suffers from such chronic underinvestment or short-term thinking in the capital markets that a pool of unexploited, high-return investments exists?

The answer to this last question is so widely assumed as true that few bother to look for the evidence. One exception is the Competitiveness Policy Council, which concluded in a recent report that there was not a persuasive case for an underinvestment problem. Many of the analysts on the Subcouncil on Financial Markets

> do not believe that any convincing evidence exists that suggests that a pervasive underinvestment problem is present in the United States, or that U.S. capital markets are characterized by short time horizons. . . . On no other issue was the Subcouncil more united than in its disagreement with this proposition.[75]

Perhaps further exploration of all these questions will yield a similar consensus on the role of government in financing the next generation of American entrepreneurs. At a minimum, the exercise should yield a firmer foundation for future policy debates.

---

[74]See the White House Report, *Aspects of High-Tech Performance,* which found the job creation role of small high-tech firms to have been exaggerated.

[75]*Report of the Subcouncils,* pp. 137, 150.

TWO

Technology Policy and Venture Capital

Anthony S. Clark

The House Science, Space, and Technology Committee of the House of Representatives is considering competitiveness legislation (the National Competitiveness Act of 1993, H.R. 820) that includes a proposal for a partnership between government and the venture capital industry. The general purpose of H.R. 820 is to improve American industrial competitiveness, create jobs, and boost economic growth by encouraging investment in a variety of technologies. The venture capital program is one tool in this plan to increase the level and rate of technology creation and adoption in response to market demands and industry needs.

Availability of Risk Capital

There are sound economic reasons for the U.S. government to promote technology commercialization and correct market failures that impede such activity. First, economists have clearly demonstrated that tech-

45

nology plays a significant role in economic development. Since World War II, from a third to a half of economic growth has been attributed to advancements in technology. Second, the social rates of return on research and development investment far exceed the private return. As a result, government subsidized investment in technology development generates substantial net returns for the economy.

Most economists agree that innovation drives economic growth. But technological development is clearly an expensive, high-risk endeavor. Congress is concerned that there is a chronic underinvestment in research and development. The prevailing climate of risk aversion in the capital markets is impeding America's long-term economic prospects by slowing the pace of innovation and technology commercialization and threatens entrepreneurial activity. President Clinton, who shares these concerns, has made national technology policy a major element of his economic package. The intent of legislation like H.R. 820 is to promote innovation and put into practice many of the principles embodied in the Clinton plan.

With that as background, let me describe the problem of risk capital in more detail. From a macroeconomic standpoint, the United States has too many liabilities and not enough assets to cover those liabilities. Accelerated consumption, deferred investment, and debt accumulation characterized economic activity during the 1980s. Chronic underinvestment in productive assets is well documented and below what the relative returns would justify. The evidence suggests that the availability of risk capital has declined. Large, established companies are replacing debt with equity and in the process are soaking up equity risk capital that was once available in the private market. Most financial institutions, largely in response to the economic trends of the 1980s, are swapping credit risk for interest-rate risk. Lending activity is down, and the volume of private placements of loans is also down.

For evidence of this shift in the allocation of risk capital, one need only look at the widening cost-of-capital spread between low-credit risks and high-credit risks. Historically, the cost of loans to small businesses has been about 150 basis points above prime. Today, they are about 270 basis points above prime. Although general lending is down, the demand for small business loans is up. Last year at the Small Business Administration's 7(a) loan program, which is the largest government loan program for small business, demand was up 35 percent.

There are also significant valuation disparities between public and private companies, which indicate that the market requires a higher rate of return on private market investment than on more liquid investments in the public capital markets.

Similar trends are evident in the venture capital industry. The industry has consolidated and matured, increasingly focusing on later-stage, lower-risk deals. In large measure, the change is due to shifts in risk tolerance, liquidity requirements, and the sources of capital. About 90 percent of professional venture capital now comes from institutions that demand liquidity and short payback periods. As a result, the size of the funds has increased, the dollar value of the average deal has increased, and there has been a shift toward later-stage transactions.

The incentive structures of venture capital funds also encourage fund managers to move to later-stage financing and larger funds. Most venture capital fund managers have call options (in the form of a "carried interest") on the funds they manage: the larger the fund, the larger the value of this call option. Compensation within the industry is, as a result, correlated with size: compensation in the larger funds is much higher for general partners than in the smaller funds with comparable investment performance.

Taken together, these forces have moved the venture capital industry away from early-stage deals toward later-stage financing. Ten years ago, maybe 50 or 60 percent of all deals were early-stage deals. Today, they are about 20 percent. Classic venture capital—that is, investing in early-stage companies—is being replaced by later-stage, merchant capital–type of activities.

A survey done by our committee of the fifty or sixty remaining early-stage funds found that the smaller funds are increasing their liquidity. When asked about cash reserves, the general response was that cash reserves today are $4 to $5 for every $1 invested. Ten years ago, the ratio was about $1 of reserves for $1 invested. The change is due partly to a phenomenon called "pay-to-play." Someone needing additional capital for an investment tries to entice other venture capital firms to participate. If a large firm participates, the cost to the entrepreneur and initial investors for the capital is often lower valuations, higher cost-of-capital, and diluted ownership.

Venture capital does not come only from professional venture capital firms but from an informal market of individual investors known as "angels," who provide from ten to twenty times more than the amount available from professional venture capitalists. But like the general capital market, the supply of risk capital from angel investors has contracted in recent years. Federal Reserve data on the flow of funds show, for example, that direct ownership of private company equity by individuals has declined proportionally by roughly 42 percent in the past five years. The asset allocation of individuals is moving toward pensions, mutual funds, and money market funds.

The weight of the evidence suggests, therefore, a significant contraction in the amount of risk capital available for technology entrepreneurs. To limit the negative effects of this capital contraction on innovation, policy makers need to examine how the government should remedy the problem of scarce risk capital for technology commercialization.

Government as a Facilitator of Venture Capital

Most competitiveness experts and economists would agree that the government should promote investment, encourage entrepreneurial activity, and preserve and strengthen the free market capital delivery system necessary for early-stage technology investing or "classic" venture capital. The debate is over how to accomplish these objectives in the most efficient and effective way. The legislation H.R. 820 takes a direct approach by investing public money in technology development to the extent justified by potential returns. As in private investment decisions, however, the private sector would make the investment decisions in the proposed program.

There are clear precedents for this program in the United States and around the world. The largest venture capital fund in the world with roughly $5 billion in assets under management is, for example, an enormously successful public-private partnership in the United Kingdom, known as 3I (Investors in Industry). When all public-private venture capital funds in the United States and throughout the world are examined, two principles characterize the successful funds:

coinvestment of public and private funds and investment decisions made solely by the private sector. H.R. 820 is based on the same principles.

Therefore, whether one agrees or disagrees with the direct approach, H.R. 820 and the venture capital provisions in the bill must be recognized as a serious and credible effort to promote economic opportunities and entrepreneurial activities in the technology sector. More efficient or effective proposals for accomplishing the same objectives are certainly welcome. Whatever the final outcome, the legislation and policy process will benefit from thorough public debates like this one.

THREE

Keep Government Out of Venture Capital

Richard Florida

A review of the evidence suggests that government involvement in venture capital is not necessary, that such involvement is not likely to succeed, and that government's scarce resources could be more effectively and efficiently used in other areas.

If the proponents of a federal venture capital program such as the one included in the National Competitiveness Act of 1993 (H.R. 820) are right, making the government a venture capitalist will generate the start-up companies, the new technologies, and the economic growth that President Clinton and Robert Reich, secretary of labor, point to as the keys to long-term prosperity. But as we say in the Midwest, where there is a lot of venture capital but not a lot of high-technology investment, the road to bigger deficits is paved with good intentions.

Those who seek to make government a venture capitalist argue that private venture capitalists and other investors are underinvesting in new start-up companies. In particular, they argue that venture capitalists are putting more of their time and money into so-called later-stage activities such as follow-on investing and leveraged buyouts (LBOs). To bridge the "capital gap," proponents conclude, the government should be involved in the venture capital business.

We Have Enough Venture Capital

Before we tackle the issue of the government's role, we need to know whether there is really a problem with the venture capital market and how much venture capital is enough.

One problem with the policy debate is that there is little evidence that the United States is underinvesting in venture capital. Venture capital investment was quite substantial even in the so-called lean years of 1990 and 1991, when the United States invested more than $3.25 billion in venture capital in more than 2,000 entrepreneurial companies. More than $330 million of that was in seed and start-up businesses. And U.S. venture capital investments rose to more than $2.2 billion in 1992, as the country began to pull out of recession.

Is this too little venture capital? In both comparative and historical terms, the answer is no. The U.S. venture capital system is, by all accounts, the envy of the world. It is our great strength. We invest more capital than our two major competitors, Japan and Germany, combined. The United States is also raising and investing more venture capital today than we ever did before. Think back to the late 1970s and the early 1980s, a period in which many of the most innovative start-up companies in the high-technology revolution were founded, companies like Intel and Apple. The

United States invested between $200 million and $600 million a year in contrast to the average of $1.4 billion invested in 1991 and 1992. U.S. venture capital investments were also up in 1992, as the country began to pull out of the recession. Activities that determine success such as the initial public offering (IPO) rate and the share of IPOs financed by venture capital also reached near record highs in 1992.

Moreover, venture capital is not the whole ballgame. Venture capitalists finance less than 1 percent of all business start-ups and about 10 percent of all high-technology start-ups, considerably more than the 2 percent figure quoted by advocates of a greater government role. Other investors include angels and informal investors such as the doctors, the dentists, the rich relatives, and so forth.

Global corporations are also starting to invest directly in high-technology start-ups and thereby provide an important new source of capital for entrepreneurs who have come to recognize the hazards of venture capital. In fact, global corporations in many cases offer a compelling alternative to venture capitalists. In the eighteen months from the beginning of 1990 through the first six months of 1991, corporations invested more than $1.4 billion directly (equity investments) in start-up companies; that was more than 50 percent of the total venture capital invested in this period. Take the multimedia industry, for example, that is, the integration of the television set, the computer, the fax machine, and digital communications. Two of the most promising start-ups in this field, Kaledia Labs and General Magic, have been funded almost entirely, not with the old-style venture capital model, but with direct investments of IBM, Apple, Sony, and Toshiba. The corporations gain because they gain access to the technology and production. The entrepreneurs like it because they do not have to give away the store.

From the entrepreneur's perspective, venture capitalists get too much for their money. They can take, for example, 51 percent of a company, dominate its board seats, and get rid of the owner. Their objective is to sell the company within five to seven years; their success in fact means selling the company. In fact, entrepreneurs refer to them as "vulture capitalists." With corporate investments, entrepreneurial companies gain instead a long-term partnership and a stream of "patient" capital for manufacturing, marketing, and distribution. Alliances between fledgling start-ups and large companies also make sense for the American economic system as a whole because they offer a way to turn new innovations into successful commercial products.

A second problem with much of the policy debate is the prevailing assumption that the United States needs as much venture capital today as it had in the mid-1980s. But do we have too little venture capital now, or did we have too much venture capital then? There is strong evidence to suggest that the United States may have had too much venture capital then. Or, as those familiar with the venture industry put it, "There was too much money chasing too few good ideas." There was a lot of cash out there but not many promising companies in which to invest.

The venture capital market virtually exploded during the 1980s. The influx of new capital brought so many new and inexperienced venture capitalists into the business that the talent base of the industry was diluted. Only 28 percent of venture capital funds in this country have one general partner or person with more than ten years of experience. Many of the new venture capitalists lacked the knowledge, the contact base, or the judgment to identify good deals. A "herd mentality" developed, where venture capitalists who could not find good new investments began to follow one another. This follow-the-leader syndrome, or what Bill Sahlman has called a "myopic capital market," meant that more start-up companies were being funded than could hope to survive in industries such as computer disk drives, notebook personal computers, or biotechnology. Devastating shakeouts and huge losses were the result.

The venture capital industry responded the way financial markets are supposed to—it corrected itself. Returns on venture capital plummeted, and investors redeployed their capital; that is why the market fell sharply in 1990 and 1991 before rebounding to more than $2 billion in 1992. According to Venture Economics, the internal rate of return for venture capital, which hovered in the range of 25 to 35 percent for funds formed in the mid-1970s and 15 to 25 percent for those formed in the early 1980s, fell to less than 5 percent for funds formed in the heyday of the mid-to-late 1980s. Yet it is this period that H.R. 820 wants to emulate—not the kind of return that, in my opinion, demands an expansion of the market.

Moreover, why should the government try? The market is already correcting itself. Market-based forces appear to be correcting what industry insiders view as the overfunding of the late 1980s. It would be an ironic mistake for government to intervene at the very time the market seems to be working.

Government Is a Poor Venture Capitalist

Even if the premise is accepted that government should get involved in the venture capital business, can the government do a good job? Does it make sense for government to become a venture capitalist?

Proponents of a federal venture capital program argue that the government has a successful track record in the venture capital business, and 3I, the U.K. venture capital fund, is cited as the example. But perhaps we should think twice about trying to emulate the United Kingdom on this. More important, consider the problematic records of two American examples: the Small Business Investment Company (SBIC) program and state venture capital programs.

People around Washington argue that the Small Business Administration's SBIC program has been a great success and should be used as the model for a federal venture capital program. SBIC was started in the late 1950s to secure capital for small businesses, but it was not such a success. Its failures are well documented, and the SBIC program is littered with mismanagement and abuse. Less than ten years after the program's inception, hundreds of SBICs went bankrupt. Today, SBICs make up just 5 percent of the venture capital, while continuing to consume considerable public capital as leverage.

The states provide a more contemporaneous example. During the 1980s, a wide range of states, my own state of Pennsylvania included, decided to create venture capital funds as part of a strategy—which ultimately failed—to develop high-technology enclaves or Silicon Valleys and Silicon Prairies. Cities like Pittsburgh would somehow be magically transformed into venture-capital and high-technology centers. By 1990, twenty-three states had established venture capital programs, consuming nearly $200 million in public capital.

What happened? Our empirical work shows that these states watched most of their locally subsidized venture capital leave for Silicon Valley in California, Route 128 around Boston, and other places with good investments, or go to local companies that failed to generate any profits. As a result, the states are pulling back from taking on the role of venture capitalist. Through my work with the state governments and the Council of Great Lakes Governors, I have come into contact with those who are now saying that "government can't do venture capital well; let the private sector do it." The states are also pulling back on their so-called "critical technology" programs.

The bottom line is basic: Government is ill equipped to deal in the high-risk, high-return world of venture capital, where tremendous profits from one or two home runs offset nine or ten strikeouts. Moreover, a public venture capital fund will likely face political pressure to invest in pet projects in key congressional districts. It is silly for government even to consider the costly business of direct financing. There are more powerful ways that government can influence the flow of capital, such as manipulating the tax rate on capital gains or liberalizing restrictions on private investors.

Venture Capital Is Not the Problem

The U.S. venture capital system for financing start-ups is not the problem or an area of weakness. Instead, the system is by every account a source of comparative advantage. Japan, Germany, and many other countries are trying to emulate how we get private venture capitalists to invest in technology start-ups.

Why does Washington consistently try to mend our strengths while ignoring our weakness? The real competitiveness problem lies downstream from innovation—in the difficulties both start-ups and large corporations have in turning new ideas and technologies into a continuous stream of quality products that people around the world want to buy. The United States leads the world in making the technological break-throughs, generating the innovations and the new in-dustrial sectors, but then fails to follow through. The problem is the "breakthrough illusion" of the U.S. in-novation system.[1] Venture capitalists create incentives for people to chase after breakthroughs or home runs rather than following through. Venture capital, espe-cially too much of it, contributes to the breakthrough illusion problem.

Another problem is that venture capitalists create powerful incentives to commercialize technology by pulling an invention out of existing companies and forming start-ups. In Silicon Valley, for example, every new idea seems to lead to the formation of a new start-up—a wasteful and inefficient process. In a system of "chronic entrepreneurship," existing firms suffer from raids and defections of key scientists, technologists, and management personnel. Promising projects are abandoned and companies find it hard to follow through on breakthroughs they have made. A delicate balance is required for our system of venture-capital-backed innovation to succeed. Too much venture capi-tal, while it may lead to more start-ups, may in fact be detrimental to the national economy.

More important, the focus on finance and on hav-ing government fill the so-called capital gaps misses the point. It diverts attention from the more funda-mental issues at hand. The United States possesses an innovative financial system; finance is where we are strong. We invent financial institutions and instru-

---

[1]Richard Florida and Martin Kenney, *The Breakthrough Illu-sion: Corporate America's Failure to Move from Innovation to Mass Production* (New York: Basic Books, 1990).

ments in ways and at a pace that exceed any of our competitors—witness our venture capital market, our futures trading, and our ability to turn mortgages into securities and trade them like stocks and bonds. No one comes even close to our ability to do this. Our financial system does a good job—an impressive job—of channeling capital to industries and sectors where the return is highest. When existing institutions and instruments fail to do this, our financial markets create new ones.

The real problem lies elsewhere—in our research and development (R&D) labs, in our factories, and in our start-up companies themselves, which produce an impressive array of breakthrough technologies but still fail to provide the follow-through required for long-term commercial success. This is something that corporations, not government, need to address.

In a nutshell, we have the equation reversed. We continue to focus attention on repairing our financial system, or our "capital allocation problem," while the real problem lies in our industrial base. Firms and managers are taking too long to restructure themselves into world-class global competitors. The United States needs to create an economic climate where individuals and firms can be more effective at harnessing the full creative capabilities of all people in the R&D lab, in the start-up company, and on the factory floor. In the Great Lakes states, we have begun redefining the technology policy debate to focus on these challenges. There are no quick fixes, but corporations, not government, have to lead.

FOUR

Don't Fix What Isn't Broken

William A. Sahlman

Before moving onto the role of government policy in entrepreneurial activity, I would like to start with three fundamental premises.

- First, I do not believe it is appropriate in our economy to create rules and regulations that favor one sector over another. The government should not favor venture capital over non-venture-capital–backed activities, high technology over low technology, manufacturing over service, or capital intensive over labor intensive. The claimed advantages of high technology or the disadvantages of low technology are in fact ephemeral and not founded on economic theory.
- Second, people behave in their own perceived best interest. This premise is basic to any discussion of government policy, if we want to infer how people are likely to behave in response to a change in the rules.
- Third, we cannot study any economic policy recommendation out of context. We need to examine the

entire picture as it relates to the fundamental goals we want to accomplish. In the case of legislation like H.R. 820, Congress needs to assess what is really going on with the entrepreneurial sector of the economy.

Role of Venture Capitalists

People often talk about two sources of capital for entrepreneurial ventures: professional venture capitalists and the so-called angels. But the venture capital share is very modest compared with the total amount of capital invested in new businesses each year. Professional venture capitalists finance roughly 2,000 companies per year; yet there are approximately 800,000 new businesses incorporated each year in the United States. Angels invest ten to twenty times more than professional capitalists.

Although often missing from the list, bootstrap financing (internally generated funds) is an important third source of financing for entrepreneurs. Hewlett-Packard, which survived and thrived on internally generated funds throughout much of its history, is just one of many bootstrap companies. The public capital market increasingly provides another important source of capital for entrepreneurs, even for those early-stage ventures without any revenue. 3DO is the most recent example.

What Shortage of Venture Capital?

Much has been made of the dip in the venture capital market from $5 billion a year to $1 billion a year. But it is not hard to imagine why the market, angel-financing included, went down. Investors expected high rates of return—20, 25, or 30 percent. They got the number right; they just got the sign wrong. It is not necessary to have a Ph.D. in economics to understand that when people start to lose money, they want to shift funds to alternative investments.

Poor rates of return led to the decline in venture capital, which in turn has recently produced prospective rates of return in venture capital that are higher than they have been in the past fifteen years. Those in the venture capital community are walking around smiling, because they are making the best deals that they have made in recent history. The IPO market has also been particularly favorable. The aggregate IPO market, excluding closed-end funds, surged from $4.5 billion in 1990 to $16.4 billion in 1991 to $24 billion last year. That is at least three times as high as the previous peak.

The United States can expect, therefore, a remarkable increase in venture capital activity. To imagine that the United States is suffering from a shortage of capital going into high-growth or high-potential ventures is simply wrong.

More Government Is Not the Answer

To understand the limits of government in entrepreneurial finance, consider the analogy of horse-and-rabbit stew. The stew has one horse and one rabbit, but the horse dominates the taste. In terms of policy, the rabbit is an attempt to induce people to do something when in fact there are fifteen or twenty other changes (the horse) that are more important in producing the desired behavior.

Imagine, for example, two entrepreneurs discussing President Clinton's proposal to lower the capital gains rate applied to investment in small business held for five years. One might turn to the other and say, "You know, Charlie, this new Clinton proposal is really exciting. I've decided to leave my job to start a new business because of this lower tax rate in five years." But although such a conversation could take place in Washington, it is unlikely to take place anywhere else in the world. It is not an accurate description of how investment decisions are made.

Tax treatment of the gains made in five years is about thirty-fifth on the list of concerns of people starting a business. Access to bank capital, which ranks much higher, is a real problem, especially for bootstrap or angel-backed companies that need bank capital to secure the working capital necessary for a successful business venture. There are no loans to small businesses. That is a real problem—a government-created problem.

Health care costs are another problem. Regulations such as the Americans with Disabilities Act and the American Family Leave Act, all of which may be appropriate social policies, have a disproportionately negative economic impact on small business. The list goes on to include litigation costs and environmental legislation. At the end of that list is whether you get a 50 percent reduction in the capital gains tax provided your total gain is less than $10 million. To focus on this "rabbit" would produce an unmitigated disaster.

Another popular and unfortunate proposal would try to encourage entrepreneurial activity with loan guarantees. Loan guarantees are already the heroin of government: the total value of outstanding guarantees in the United States is more than $6 trillion. Loan guarantees are designed to provide incentives for some set of activities, such as the SBICs or the new venture capital program proposed in H.R. 820. My experience with loan guarantees has taught me the importance of going back to first principles—people will behave in their own best interests. Who will behave differently as a result of access to a pool of taxpayer-financed venture capital, and do we really need to change that behavior? There is not one shred of evidence that professional, well-managed venture capitalists need access to government loan guarantees. What they need is better rates of return. If they have better rates of return, they will get all the money they ever wanted.

In conclusion, the United States does not need new policies such as those described in the venture capital legislation now before Congress. Irrespective of government policy and the decisions made in Washington on this legislation, the future for venture capital is bright. The market can also be expected to continue to move to meet whatever new challenges may arise.

FIVE

Where Do We Go from Here?
A Discussion

QUESTION: As Richard Florida mentioned, the United States has a problem with follow-through on innovations. The solution is to create a better business climate, but how should this be done?

ANTHONY S. CLARK, House Committee on Science, Space, and Technology: Whether with government venture capital programs or tax policy, we have a constant need to balance a variety of opinions and options. The tension can be seen in the 1986 tax reform. Congress tried to promote the efficient allocation of capital by taxing all income at the same level. But many policy makers consider the tax code an effective instrument to achieve social goals, which may not be driven by economic considerations.

On venture capital, Bill Sahlman takes the position similar to the no-intervention policy embodied the 1986 Tax Act. Those who take that position should not favor any cut in the capital gains tax. I agree with him that a cut may not have a significant effect on investment practices or on America's long-run economic prospects.

I would argue that venture capital peaked in the mid-1980s because of government deregulation of the Employment Retirement Income Security Act (ERISA) rules that allowed pensions to invest in venture capital funds. It is interesting to note, however, that of the $4 billion committed to venture capital in 1984, roughly $2 billion went to two LBO funds.

I think Bill Sahlman is also right in his observation that most venture capitalists are pleased at the moment, because they are seeing the best valuations in ten years. The returns on those investments should be very good. Although money is going into that industry because of those prospects, most of that money is going to larger funds and later-stage financing of existing ventures, creating an imperfect allocation of risk capital.

Our real problem is in the early-stage segment of the venture capital market. This gap in financing early-stage ventures is caused by the institutional injection of venture capital and by an imperfect flow of information that is particularly evident in the informal angel market. Venture capitalists perform a key screening role as they examine the never-ending stream of business plans that cross their desks. But fewer and fewer early-stage deals are being reviewed and assessed by professionals, a situation that suggests an increase in the inefficiency in this segment of the market.

Proposals such as the venture capital program in H.R. 820 are intended to bridge this capital gap, lower the cost of venture capital for early-stage technology companies, and improve the prospective rate of innovation. The user cost of capital in this market segment is very high. As a result, the United States will get fewer start-ups, fewer attempts at innovating, and ultimately a lower rate and level of innovation.

WILLIAM SAHLMAN, Harvard Business School: On this presumed deficit in early-stage ventures, I have what I call the field-of-dreams theory: if there is a shortage, investors will come. If there are high prospective rates of return, I have great faith that my colleagues in the investment community will figure it out, move to capture those returns, and the market will correct itself.

Improving the performance of small business and entrepreneurship is not any more important than improving the performance of large and established companies such as General Motors, IBM, and Motorola. As for competitiveness over the past ten to twenty years, business was fairly easy. The United States had high market share in many sectors of the economy. But a fair amount of fat crept into the system, in part because fat always creeps into the system when there are not competitive challenges. Confronted with two fundamental challenges, large companies did not do well. The first, the entrepreneurial revolution, was like a slap in the face: people started companies out of nowhere that changed the very structure of the economy. The second, and perhaps even more important, challenge was the sudden rise of competitive trading partners. Parts of the world that had not been competitive before challenged the United States in a variety of different markets. Japan provided the most prominent example in the extended learning process the United States had to undergo.

The new challenges do not mean, as some have argued, that the key to continued prosperity lies with the promotion of the entrepreneurial sector that did so well at the expense of our large-company sector in the late 1970s and early 1980s. Indeed, to encourage one part of the system at the expense of another part is misguided and wrong.

Moreover, rather than worrying about the capital gains rate, we need to focus on changing our system that currently penalizes savings and encourages consumption. If President Clinton is successful in lowering the capital gains rate on investments held five years, how many people would be willing to bet that five years later they will have a lower tax rate applied to gains they make in any sector of the economy? My own view is this is a sucker's bet.

If we want to reduce the cost of capital in the United States relative to other parts of the world, then we need to reduce, or at least not increase, uncertainty. I believe the uncertainty about government policy and the concern about the direction under Clinton increase the cost of capital by 2 or 3 percent, swamping any presumed difference that exists among Germany, Japan, and the United States.

RICHARD FLORIDA, Carnegie Mellon University: Mr. Clark and sponsors of competitiveness legislation often start with the intention of improving the business climate for commercialization, but the proposals and supporting arguments end up focused on the innovation side of the equation.

Many good intentions about getting the economy moving are behind the legislation and the plan to get the government into the venture capital business, but a key assumption behind both moves has been overlooked. Do we really believe that new technology and innovations will save the United States? Do we really believe that seed and start-up companies are the engines of the innovation process? The plan in H.R. 820 or S. 4 sounds good: develop critical technologies, involve government, move the technologies out of the laboratory, and get start-ups going.

70

But even if we assume that the plan will be a big success, what will be accomplished? More innovations. From an economic perspective, the "rents" from innovation pale, however, in comparison with the continuous stream of value from producing successful commercial products. Value is created, wealth is generated, and productivity is improved when quality products are produced that people want to buy in world markets. Do we really want to create incentives for more breakthroughs at the expense of doing other things that both corporations and the government need to do? I think not.

WILLIAM S. HARAF, Citicorp: When making the case for a government role in the marketplace, proponents refer to two types of market failure. One is that capital markets have imperfections that discourage venture capital investments. It may be that there is too much risk aversion, as Tony Clark suggested, or insufficient information on investment opportunities. Both Richard Florida and Bill Sahlman addressed these potential problems.

The market failure that has not been addressed is the social return to investment that exceeds the private sector return for certain types of investments. For those investments, there is a potential role for government financing. Do you believe that such investments are prevalent in the market? And would a proposal such as the federal venture capital program take care of the problem?

MR. SAHLMAN: There may very well be pockets in the economy where the social return far exceeds the private return. But it is difficult to get to them. It is not at all clear that those disparities between social and private return can be captured through government policy. If we try to address those problems, we often create unintended costs elsewhere. Again, I provide the example of the SBIC program or loan guarantees. The program attracted a tremendous number of promoters who were not necessarily skilled at venture capital investing but who were extremely skilled at management fee collection and raising capital.

There may be market failures and circumstances under which loan guarantees or a program to encourage venture capital would be appropriate. I see, however, no evidence of them, and I am fairly sure the government cannot find them.

MR. FLORIDA: The question refers to the classic argument for direct government investment in technology and basic R&D: R&D has significant social benefits, but firms will not invest because of the risk or the distant payoff, so government needs to pump money into R&D projects.

While many economists take this as "natural law," it is not. In fact, this argument has its roots in history, not in a natural law. It is part of the cold war economy that the United States and other countries built after World War II. Government now influences the economy in innumerable ways. Identifying special activities, selecting particular technologies to support, and pumping money collected through tax revenues into them are probably the most costly and inefficient ways the government affects the economy. As Bill Sahlman mentioned, the government also weighs in on the economy through regulation and various financial incentives.

The real problem today is not that the government is doing too little but that it is doing far too much to influence the economy. We have developed a layer cake of government programs over the past fifty years to meet the so-called needs of specific sectors and specific constituencies. This layer cake contains R&D programs, economic policies, financial regulations, environmental regulations, labor and social policies, and the like. Now government through H.R. 820, S. 4, and other measures wants to add yet another layer of icing to this layer cake. This, however, can only "harden" the cake, which is already collapsing under its own weight.

All this activity may have been useful in the old economy. But the United States has gone through a fairly fundamental economic transformation. The first wave was marked by entrepreneurial firms such as Apple, Intel, Microsoft, and Sun Microsystems. The second wave witnessed the rise of off-shore competitors, particularly in Asia, who changed the rules of manufacturing with new techniques that emphasized teams, quality, and just-in-time supply.

In this emerging economy, the fundamental principles are quite different from the old cold war economy. In the old economy, wealth creation hinged on taking physical labor and turning it into productivity advances. The new economy hinges on turning knowledge and brainpower into value, making the old system irrelevant or at best a problem.

The Clinton administration and the Congress could do the American people a big favor by focusing on the real issues. We must start not with ways to put more icing on the layer cake but with ways to take the layer cake apart. How do we begin to pull apart systematically the disincentives, the problems, and the programs that may have had a role in the old economy but that now impair the functioning of the new one? This is the issue that federal policy must begin to address.

MR. CLARK: Before we tackle how to manage business and the economy responsibly in the post–cold war period, keep in mind the Johnstown, Pennsylvania, flood of the late 1880s. Although the people in Johnstown implored the owners of the lake overlooking the town to shore up their dam, the owners replied, "Forget it. Don't worry." The flood burst the dam following torrential rains, and 2,000 people were killed.

The lesson of the Johnstown flood is that just because people are in a position to act responsibly does not mean that they will. And that is what has occurred in the banking industry: the proliferation of LBOs, speculative loans, and excessive risk and speculation. Management did not fully weigh the long-term risks. Government is needed, therefore, to look beyond cyclical events to take into account long-term secular trends. Otherwise, financial chaos may result.

MR. FLORIDA: I agree with Tony Clark that government has a role to play. Private economic actors and financial markets act within the context and structure of incentives that governments help construct. The issue is what the incentive structure and new policy environment should look like.

The Great Lakes states may offer some examples of where to go and, just as important, what to avoid. I am working with the Council of Great Lakes Governors, a consortium of the eight states that border the Great Lakes: New York, Pennsylvania, Ohio, Indiana, Illinois, Michigan, Minnesota, and Wisconsin. We are exploring what is needed for high-quality, high-performance manufacturing to flourish in the United States. This entire industrial heartland region has seen a significant economic rebound over the past decade. One lesson is that public venture capital programs are not necessary and may actually slow economic development.

Many policy makers still see places like Silicon Valley in California or Route 128 around Boston as the drivers of the American economy and as the model for entrepreneurship in high technology. H.R. 820 is one proposal, for example, intended to promote this model and export it to other regions of the country. But what has happened is that many of the Great Lakes states are already reindustrializing. Under intense market pressure, companies like Xerox, Motorola, and Steelcase (the office furniture maker) are transforming themselves into global leaders as they develop new business methods and manufacturing techniques. Foreign investors and Japanese transplants have also played a central role in helping to transform this region. In spite of the failed venture capital and critical technology programs, the state economies turned around. Why? The transformation is due to a more fundamental shift to a new "high-performance" system of manufacturing and economic organization.

The hundreds of high-performance quality firms are now demanding change from the governors such as an educational system that turns out people who can read and write as well as work in teams. We are told at Carnegie Mellon, as I am sure Bill Sahlman has been told at Harvard Business School, that we turn out people who work well as individuals but not as team players. The companies complain that our graduates come into their company and disrupt the teams that they have spent ten years setting up. We are now developing new educational programs to address this problem. New types of infrastructure investments are also needed. The United States has created a highway system that encourages suburbanization: move out and travel. The problem is that congested highways and decentralized activity conflict with new trends in manufacturing toward just-in-time delivery. Command-and-control environmental regulations are still another obstacle. And the list goes on and on.

ROBERT REAGAN, National Society of Professional Engineers: If there is plenty of venture capital, why are our members of the National Society of Professional Engineers saying they cannot get any of this capital? There must be a disconnect somewhere, if these small business entrepreneurs who are starting their own companies and have good ideas cannot get the necessary financing. What other factors determine who gets the money and who does not?

MR. SAHLMAN: Commercial success requires much more than inventions and ideas. Unless an invention is married to a management team that can bring it to commercial fruition and create a substantive company, it will not attract capital. In California, these cases used to be called MIT deals: a scientist and nothing else. A California deal was a complete management team and a scientist. Over time, the supply of managers willing to work with people who have good ideas has increased dramatically. When someone puts the idea together with the managerial resources required to create value, the capital flows. Even if we include the time when the venture capital market was down, I have yet to see an idea that should get financing fail to get it. But I have seen many ideas financed that should not have been financed. Maybe that is an idiosyncratic view of the world, but it reflects reality as I see it.

My experience with inventors is that they do not value the commercial skills of managers. Only when they believe that without that marriage they will not get capital or the rents associated with their invention will the logjam break. It is often a choice. Entrepreneurs say, "I don't want to give up 51 percent," or "I don't want to have a manager. The idea is so good; why won't people invest?" People will not invest because the hit rate is approximately zero.

MR. FLORIDA: I want to emphasize the need to get the incentive structure right. We spend tens of billions of dollars of federal money to create inventions that for the most part do not have a market. Researchers in federal labs, R&D units, corporate R&D units, and universities are told that their job is to invent and to create more technology, no matter what is done with it.

The result is an incentive system that rewards people for inventions: if you make a better mousetrap, the world will beat a path to your door. But the hard work is developing the market, creating the management team, and developing the ability to sell the commercial product in the marketplace.

MR. REAGAN: As rates of return fell, investors were, of course, less interested in contributing to venture capital markets. Is there something that should be done to address the decline in the rates of return on venture capital so that they become stable again?

MR. CLARK: Improving the rate of return on investment has absolutely nothing to do with the availability or cost of capital. The return on investment is essentially a function of the net present value of the cash flows of the enterprise, which are determined by sales, earnings, and ultimately market demand. A good product will get sales and attract capital.

In the venture capital industry, the partition between early and later stages is now determined by market demand as reflected in sales trends. In the product stage of the cycle, the entrepreneur has already developed product prototypes, tested the market, and made some initial sales. The professional venture capitalist examines the initial sales rate to determine if the prospective return warrants his investment.

The entrepreneur's problem is getting ideas to the point that potential investors can judge the market outlook. That is the concern. Richard Florida and Bill Sahlman made the distinction between large and small companies. That is not the concern of H.R. 820, and it is not the intent of the bill's sponsors to favor one or the other. Instead, the intent is to recognize that the innovations of both small and large companies contribute significantly to economic development.

The problem of inadequate financing for start-ups also generates potential market failures with radical innovations. There are two types of innovation: component innovation and architectural innovation. Component innovation takes an existing product and improves it to satisfy existing customer needs better. Most of those innovations are developed by established large companies. When a large company makes a "strategic acquisition" of another company, it is generally looking for a component innovation to complement its product line and thereby meet the demands of its customers better.

The architectural innovation is a new product that does not have a developed market. These innovations are typically developed by start-up firms, because the start-up is not captive to an existing customer base. A start-up is well suited to the task for two reasons: it has a new product and a virgin market plus a hunger to develop that market. With fewer start-ups, we get fewer attempts at architectural innovation, which in turn could slow or yield a less than socially desirable pace of technological advance.

HOWARD GLECKMAN, *Business Week*: The Clinton administration seems to have its eye on pension funds as a source of financing for many projects: low-income housing, infrastructure, and the rest. What are the risks and rewards of the government's providing incentives or disincentives to invest in venture projects?

MR. CLARK: An inherent conflict exists in using pension fund money to achieve social goals. The pension fund is a fiduciary that acts on behalf of its beneficiaries. It has a legal requirement, first and foremost, to act in a prudent investment manner on behalf of its beneficiaries. The conflict arises when government tries to affect the investment behavior of a pension fund to meet some social goal that is not driven by return on investments for the benefit of the beneficiaries of that pension fund.

MR. SAHLMAN: In practice, government and pension funds are like the *Exxon Valdez*. You may recall the *Valdez* headed down the channel, got off track, and then ended up on a reef. The captain and crew immediately attempted to pull the ship off the reef, which had the unintended effect of maximizing the spillage of oil.

Pension funds, like the *Exxon Valdez*, have a history of overcommitting to certain sectors of the economy—venture capital, real estate, small stocks, and foreign stocks are but a few of the examples. They invest in search of higher returns, but when the returns are disappointing, they withdraw, thereby driving returns even lower. I am not enthusiastic, therefore, about pension funds allocating capital—public or private. In fact, I am scared to death.

There is $4 trillion in pension funds and insurance funds in the United States. Money moves very rapidly in response to perceived higher rates of return, causing significant fluctuation in the cost of capital and the allocation of capital. When pension funds move, they almost always destroy the perceived higher rates of return that they sought to earn in the first place. Real estate is the most prominent example.

JEANETTE SMITH, National Association of Small Business Investment Companies: The SBIC has had its share of rotten apples. The structure of the program was fundamentally flawed from its inception in 1958. But on September 4, 1992, President Bush signed a critical piece of legislation that changed the structure of the program. Instead of trying to provide long-term "patient" capital with debt, the focus under the new structure is now on equity.

MR. FLORIDA: Your point is well taken. The SBIC program was started in an attempt to stimulate investment in small businesses. Back in the 1950s and early 1960s, the United States did not have a professional venture capital market like the one we have today. The SBIC program was an attempt to create public venture capital funds. Ultimately, the United States learned from SBICs and tried other vehicles. The limited partnership emerged as a particularly useful institutional tool to deal with the risk-return problem: outside investors are limited partners with limited liability. It is good that the SBIC program, under the reforms of the Bush administration, is finally beginning to resemble more closely a limited partnership.

But I chose to focus on the early SBIC program in my previous comments, because it is this plan that advocates of a new federal venture capital program, such as the sponsors of the competitiveness bill, hold up as a model of success that should be emulated despite its failures. Unfortunately, even with recent reforms, it is not.

MR. SAHLMAN: The core issue regarding the SBICs is not whether they had to repay some interest on the loans that they got to support investments in venture capital. The problem is, and continues to be, the guarantee. Any time a guarantee is used, perverse incentives are created that generate negative unintended consequences.

Although I can point to SBICs that have been fabulously successful at investing in new companies—such as Apple Computer—that is not a case for public funding. Apple and the others would have gotten the money anyway without the guarantee. The investors in Apple were Arthur Rocke, Harry Singleton from Teledyne, Mike Markula from Intel Corporation, and Peter Crisp from Venrock. I would have invested. Anybody would have invested. It was a world-class management team.

The question, therefore, that policy makers need to ask is whether the government should be in the business of providing guarantees to invest in new ventures. For those projects under the program that merit support on the basis of economic criteria, would money be available on a private basis? I assert that it would. I also assert that any time anything is guaranteed—loans, capital—an incentive problem is created down the road.

MR. CLARK: But it is my understanding the SBIC is not a guarantee program. We are not talking about the Small Business Administration (SBA) loan programs. Can we define an SBIC?

ANSWER: MS. SMITH: An SBIC has met certain criteria set by the SBA SBIC program. They have raised a certain amount of private capital that can be matched by the federal government, matched not by federal direct investment but through debentures guaranteed by the federal government.

MR. SAHLMAN: I thought there was a guarantee somewhere in there, and we found it.

TOM SHEEHAN, Western Technology: What do the panelists see as the likely value of the so-called cooperative research and development agreements (CRADAs)? In a CRADA, a company puts up its share of the money and the national lab works alongside. No money changes hands, but the job gets done. Could you comment on whether you believe CRADAs will become more important, or do you think they will fizzle out?

MR. CLARK: I believe CRADAs can work quite well. But in the end, experience will show whether they are successful.

From an economic standpoint, they make sense because CRADAs are a technology risk-sharing arrangement. In a CRADA, a company is using the skills and resources of the federal government in the course of developing some technology. In the process, the government reduces overhead costs and shares the risk in developing those kinds of technologies that require large amounts of money over a long time.

MR. FLORIDA: CRADAs sound good, but they are at best a bandaid approach to a serious problem, another example of putting more icing on the layer cake. At a recent conference that I attended in Pittsburgh, quite a number of CRADAs were signed. The keynote speaker—

Dexter Baker, CEO of Air Products—put forward a very novel proposal. He turned the CRADA issue around and said, "Let's not see what we can do for the federal labs that have consumed tens of billions of taxpayer dollars annually. Let's create a 'Federal Lab Closing Commission' and let's make the federal labs show that they're worth keeping open. If they can prove that they're worth keeping open, they can meet the test of the market; we'll keep them in place. If not, shut them down." I tend to agree with that approach.

MARTHA HARRIS, National Research Council: The trend of large companies investing in small companies is quite interesting for several reasons. One, the support of the large company can help in a situation when, for instance, a small company has brought an idea to the commercialization stage but then faces bankruptcy. Two, the relationships among large and small firms are important for building and preserving a technology and economic base. What can be done to create more links between small and large firms?

MR. CLARK: Corporations are clearly investing more and more in the stock of other companies. Based on Federal Reserve and IRS data, over the past ten years the percentage of assets on corporate balance sheets invested in other companies has increased from about 10 percent to roughly 15 percent, compared with a compounded annual growth of 6 percent in all assets.

This trend suggests that established companies, by and large, may be displacing their own in-house research and development activities. Look at IBM and the Digital Equipment Corporation: they are ranked second and fifth in the United States in the magnitude of research conducted by a corporation, with IBM doing $6 billion and DEC $1.5 billion. They are slashing in-house research and, I suspect, broadening their access to technology through strategic alliances with other firms.

A particularly useful illustration is the long-distance telecommunication market, which is made up of AT&T, Sprint, and MCI. For strategic reasons, Sprint and MCI will not develop any technology in-house or do any manufacturing because they want access to technology from any source in the world that will give them a competitive edge. AT&T, by contrast, does its own in-house research and its own manufacturing; speculation on the street is that AT&T may seek to sell its manufacturing operations. I believe the corporate trend, therefore, is in the direction of greater access to a wider range of technology options.

MR. FLORIDA: The short answer to your question is, If we really want to encourage more cross investment between small and large firms, government should not get into the venture capital business. It can be healthy for corporations to invest more in entrepreneurial firms, and it helps to fashion stable, durable partnerships. The investment can provide the small company a long-term stream of capital, and it can give the corporations a stream of new innovations on which they can provide the follow-on and the marketing. This is all contingent, of course, on the large company's not stifling the innovative capabilities of the entrepreneurial partner, which has happened frequently in the past.

I believe, however, that the overfunding of the venture capital market has kept this type of cross investment and alliance building from happening more in the past. Now that we have a market correction, the investment side is working out much better. There is

DISCUSSION

absolutely no need for the federal government to get involved.

MR. SAHLMAN: On the issue of IBM's $6 billion, why do you think management is slashing it? The investment had no return. It was not a question of social return or private return. The fact is that the $6 billion was an unmitigated nightmare of inefficiency. The $2 billion or $3 billion that went into venture capital had a far higher success rate than did IBM's in-house research.

Going back to my first premise, I favor neither small firms over the IBMs of this world nor large firms over small. The focus should instead be on the fundamental managerial crisis in the United States that is in the process of resolution as managers are forced to respond to the increased demands of the competitive environment.

For big companies, the challenge is to improve performance. There are many innovations that should have taken place inside large companies and that should have been commercialized inside large companies. Indeed, in many instances, the entrepreneurial ventures that ultimately proved to be successful were first proposed inside a large company but were then rejected. That is a tragedy in many ways for the owners and employees of the large company. There are also significant transaction costs associated with leaving and starting a new venture.

The market has responded, however, to meet the new challenge. Increasingly, large firms are involved in a wide range of relationships with small companies doing research that might help fill the pipeline of the large company. The example of Merck's investments in various biotech companies is a compelling illustration of a market response to a problem of in-house innova-

85

tion. Merck has used outside efforts to create competition to its own internal R&D efforts. That very sensible approach will no doubt continue.

MR. CLARK: I agree with Bill. But I have an important follow-up point to make. At one point, IBM owned DOS but later gave it up to Microsoft. Microsoft currently has a higher market value than IBM. At one point, IBM also owned 25 percent of Intel but sold that holding. If IBM had those two products today, the operating system and the microprocessor, it would control the global personal computer market. Xerox is another example. At one point, Xerox owned Apple and Adobe, which came out with the Postscript language (the standard operating system for laser printers). As we all know, the progress in those two markets has been remarkable.

These cases illustrate what is happening in corporate in-house R&D and the valuable role small companies serve in developing innovative architectural products and new markets.

MR. SAHLMAN: But maybe the corporations made mistakes because the potential innovations threatened their existing businesses. I do not see that these "mistakes" are necessarily a problem for the marketplace or for the economy.

MR. CLARK: Neither do I. But I am responding to the point Rich Florida made earlier that we are overemphasizing or overencouraging entrepreneurial activity in start-ups. My real-world examples demonstrate the profound economic contributions that result from start-ups.

MR. FLORIDA: This is a very important issue, but it's improperly framed. Maybe it was not a mistake for IBM not to "own" DOS. Maybe it is not a mistake that IBM does not own Intel's microprocessor capability or that Xerox does not own Apple-like personal computer technology. Otherwise, we may not have those companies to point to as success stories. In an era of rapid, continuous innovation, the traditional hierarchical and bureaucratic corporation may be ill-equipped to meet the tests of both rapid technological change and increased market competition.

Let us focus on the bigger picture for a moment. In this country, we have a continuing, and sometimes expensive, discourse on our capital allocation problem. Bill Sahlman's point about capital flowing toward an attractive rate of return hits the nail right on the head. If a managerial crisis arises in the steel industry, as we have had in the United States, investors simply will not invest. If some U.S. auto companies want to stay organized along outmoded lines as we move into the twenty-first century and if these companies do not want to improve and do what it takes to be state of the art, then it is no surprise that money flows into venture capital rather than into those businesses. It is no surprise that U.S. investors put money into housing speculation or that they export their capital to other countries. That's where the return is. Capital follows productivity, wealth, and value creation, not the other way around.

The real problem lies in management's failure—given the government incentive structure—to do what it takes to become productive and competitive. It is not a capital allocation problem, but a value-creation and productivity problem. And the real surprise has been how slowly firms have responded to the new challenges.

EDWARD J. BURGER, Institute for Health Policy Analysis: Let me address an issue that has been discussed tangentially but not directly. As text for the sermon, I will take the biotechnology sector.

The amount of time, investment, and effort that has to be put into biotech to produce a rate of return and a marketable product is often substantially longer than the patience of any investor: venture capitalists, pension fund managers, or other public and private investors. That presents a significant paradox and a problem.

If, indeed, there is virtue in encouraging a longer-term view of American industry and biotech in particular, then policy makers have to consider how to achieve that objective in ways that the market itself cannot.

There are substantial imperfections as the market operates for the biotech sector, for example, that do not seem to be spontaneously amendable by Adam Smith's theories. The initial public offering experience is perverse in strange ways. The persuasions of the investment community to take up biotech are based on matters in many cases that have nothing to do with the inherent value of that sector. Once the companies are adopted and given a market value, they fall off the screen, in effect, because there is not enough activity to sustain them.

MR. SAHLMAN: In biotech, as in other sectors, people often talk about a cost-of-capital disadvantage in the United States. But I can point to a number of cases over the past ten years in the biotechnology business in which the cost of capital has clearly been negative and entrepreneurs were given capital despite an antici-pated negative rate of return.

We have had the most successful financing vehicle imaginable for biotechnology. It just happens to look like a roller coaster that periodically overvalues and undervalues biotech businesses. On average, the system may never get the value right, but there is not a shortage of capital going into the sector.

What we are experiencing, however, is a dramatic shift in people's opinions about what biotechnology, or the pharmaceutical industry, is doing. There have been allegations, for example, of price gouging. My own perspective is that there may have been price gouging. But more important, biotechnology is designed to replace the process that enables price gouging at all.

In biotech, we are moving toward a system in which the factory is not a physical factory of bricks and mortar, but a factory inside the human body. The cost of this new approach to health issues is lower and the efficacy higher than the old pharmaceutical model. The high current rates of return in the pharmaceutical industry invite innovation and encourage entry by biotechnology companies. New entry by these firms will drive down rates of return and increase the pace of innovation. Anything we do to discourage entry, which is what we do when policy pronouncements in one fell swoop lower the market value of all companies including biotechnology firms, aggravates the problem. Entry is what will solve that part of the health care problem.

MR. BURGER: But you did not address my point. What matters is the stability of the investment over a long time that may have nothing to do with the character of the pharmaceutical sector or the health care industry or the pricing of products. It is the stability of the investment, with a long-term view, that biotech deserves and needs.

MR. CLARK: In biotech, I do not perceive any problem raising money based on the relatively high stock values of publicly traded biotech companies. But individual investors should understand what is occurring in this industry. Big pensions are buying portfolios of biotech companies, looking at each company as a product. Some will succeed; others will fail. Whenever there is any whiff of a product's prospects diminishing, however, the institutions sell the stock and drive its price quickly lower.

BRAD BOTTWIN, Department of Commerce: What role does foreign venture capital play in our market? And what are the negative or positive implications for it in the future?

MR. SAHLMAN: I am not concerned about foreign venture capital or the fact that capital comes from another country and is invested in companies here. I have no problem with that, per se. I am much more concerned about what foreigners do offshore in intellectual property. We have not been diligent as a country in our policy of protecting intellectual property globally.

MR. FLORIDA: Foreign capital is a good thing in all but the most exceptional of cases. Whenever a company can get a source of capital to invest in it, it is a good thing. Even to try to make the argument that foreign capital is a problem seems to me to verge on the ludicrous. In fact, it seems contradictory to say as the Clinton administration does that we have a financing problem and then try to restrict a source of capital.

Moreover, in this era when nearly everyone in Washington appears ready to strike out at "the foreign investors that are buying our venture capital start-ups" or "the foreign investors for investing in U.S. companies," two facts are worth keeping in mind. One, foreign investors are not a major player in the venture capital market. Two, the foreigners are pulling out in response to poor returns. Japanese investments in venture capital funds went from $82 million to near zero over the 1990–1992 period. Last year, the total net foreign direct investment position for the United States was negative. Instead of groaning about the "foreigners buying up our country," we should be asking what happens when they stop investing or pull out.

MARK DESANTIS, Institute of Electrical Electronics Engineers: On Tony Clark's comment about IBM letting go of DOS, I am reminded of an earlier story about the NCR Corporation.

The president of NCR was approached by one of his vice presidents with an idea for a punch card with information and he said, "We can't do anything like that. We're in the mechanical cash register business." And he promptly fired Thomas Watson, Sr., who then went on to start IBM. A vice president that came to the president of NCR with an idea for a copying machine was also fired because of his crackpot idea. This gentleman later founded Xerox. The point is that "strategic mistakes" are the nature of business and an inherent part of the dynamic that generates start-ups. It is therefore impossible to conclude from IBM's strategic mistakes that the government needs to intervene.

On a different topic, could you discuss the issue of "patient" versus "impatient" capital? Bill Sahlman seemed to suggest that the so-called impatient capital problem is largely fiction and that American businesses have failed because of failures in business leadership and management.

MR. SAHLMAN: I am convinced that almost always when we have met the enemy, he is us and often the problem is one of management. Many of the problems were the result of managers' trying to protect the status quo rather than engaging in a process of creative self-destruction that markets ultimately demand.

On the question of how we should get the economy moving forward, I believe there are already natural forces in place that are improving the outlook. Typically, when we try to create a new policy, we take a snapshot of the economy and ignore the entire moving picture. Yet the moving picture suggests American business is increasingly competitive and capable globally. The change is a natural response to the wake-up calls managers are getting time and time again as they watch their colleagues get fired or lose market share.

When we look at the moving picture, it is very favorable for the United States—in direct contrast to a quite unfavorable moving picture for Japan and Germany. The business environment in both countries creates a considerable pipeline problem, while the United States has a much better mixture of entrepreneurship and large company dynamism promising a brighter future for the economy. Japan and Germany wish they had our venture capital business. In these countries, there is no venture capital, no entrepreneurship. The social and economic consequences of failure are so horrendous that all start-ups have stopped for the past twenty or thirty years. In Japan, someone who leaves a large company to start a small one and fails can become a bank guard—probably in another country. In Germany, someone who starts a company and fails is legally precluded from becoming the managing director in any other enterprise.

MR. CLARK: According to Federal Reserve data, an increasing percentage of investment dollars is being managed by professional money managers that have liquidity requirements and are judged on a quarterly basis. This shift to institutional money management has caused a much shorter investment time horizon. In an attempt to promote long-term investing and greater economic returns, you see the emergence of the relationship investing that Bill and I were talking about earlier. In this type of investing, people like Warren Buffet and the Bass brothers buy significant blocks of corporate stock and go on the board of directors. They become actively engaged in the affairs of a company to ensure they take the long-term investment perspective necessary for achieving and sustaining competitive advantage. My point is that the institutionalization of sources of investment capital have created enormous pressure on corporations to maximize near-term earnings and forgo long-term investment, even though such investment offers greater returns. By definition, economists would identify this behavior as a market failure that savvy investors, like Buffet, recognize.

MR. SAHLMAN: But pension funds and insurance companies typically have very long investment horizons. They take a long horizon because they like to match their assets to the structure of their liabilities. They have been doing that for a long time, investing in long-term projects. It seems to me you are suggesting that somehow they are not doing a very good job and that they are not addressing the fundamental aspect of their business, in which they have been engaged for decades.

MR. CLARK: If there is one source of long-term capital, it should be pension funds, 401(K)s, or individual retirement accounts (IRAs), because the beneficiaries do not need their money until they retire. Unfortunately, the managers of those funds are being judged by their employers quarterly. Human nature being what it is, the managers want to show the best performance. Because if they do not perform well quarterly, then they will have less money under management and thereby diminish their personal compensation.

MR. SAHLMAN: If there were a higher return over the longer time horizon, then we would see a dramatic shift in the amount of capital going into longer time-horizon investments. That is what is happening today and will likely continue over the next two years in venture capital. I believe, therefore, that the alleged time-horizon problem is again partly the problem of using a snapshot instead of a moving picture to judge the path of the economy.

LEGISLATIVE IMPACT ON VENTURE CAPITAL INVESTMENT, 1958–1993

Act	Goals
Small Business Act of 1958	Increased the availability of venture capital for small business.
1978 Revenue Act	Provided capital gains tax incentive for equity investments. Capital committed increased by $556 million from previous year.
ERISA's "Prudent Man" Rule (1979)	Clarified investment guidelines for pension investors to allow higher-risk investments.
ERISA's "Safe Harbor" Regulation (1980)	Stated that venture managers would not be considered fiduciaries of plan assets.
Economic Recovery Tax Act (1981)	Lowered capital gains rate. Capital commitments doubled to $1.3 billion in 1981.

(Table continues)

Act	Goals
Tax Reform Act of 1986	Reduced incentive for long-term capital gains.
Small Business Credit Enhancement Act of 1992	Overhauled SBIC program to shift focus from debt to equity financing.
National Competitiveness Act of 1993 (H.R. 820; S. 4)[a]	Established a venture capital program in the Commerce Department to finance high-tech start-ups.

a. Pending approval of the Senate and the Joint Conference Committee.
SOURCE: Author and T. A. Soja and J. E. Reyes, *Investment Benchmarks: Venture Capital* (Needham, Mass.: Venture Economics, Inc., 1990), p. 202.

H.R. 820

(103D CONGRESS, FIRST SESSION)

IN THE HOUSE OF REPRESENTATIVES

February 4, 1993
Mr. Valentine (for himself, Mr. Brown, et al.)

TITLE III—CRITICAL TECHNOLOGIES

Civilian Technology Development Program

(a) ESTABLISHMENT.—There is established within the Technology Administration of the Department of Commerce a national program to stimulate and supplement the availability of long-term investment capital for the formation, development, and growth of qualified business concerns throughout the United States. The Secretary, through the Under Secretary, shall, through such program, provide for the selection, licensing, monitoring, and financial and technical support of professionally managed technology investment companies which in turn shall provide financial, management, and technical assistance to qualified business concerns, with preference given to satisfying the seed and early-stage financing needs of such concerns that are not being met by other sources on reasonable terms. . . .

(1) to contribute to United States economic competitiveness, employment, and prosperity;

(2) to promote the advancement, maturation, and application of critical and other advanced technologies;

(3) to supplement and stimulate long-term investment in qualified business concerns; and

(4) to encourage and facilitate the formation and growth of professionally managed technology investment companies throughout the United States that will give preference to satisfying the capital needs of qualified business concerns, especially during their early stages of development. . . .

(e) OUTREACH TO ECONOMICALLY DEPRESSED AREAS.—The Secretary, acting through the Under Secretary, shall seek to ensure that qualified business concerns located in areas determined by the Secretary to have a depressed economy, or a significant concentration of defense-related industries, or chronically high unemployment, are notified of the availability of financial assistance through the program established under this subtitle and, to the extent practicable, to encourage and facilitate the participation of such qualified business concerns in such program.

(f) EFFECTIVE DATE.—Except as provided in subsection (d) and in sections 344 and 351(a), the provisions of this subtitle shall take effect on October 1, 1994.

(a) ESTABLISHMENT.—There is established a Civilian Technology Development Advisory Committee to be composed of 7 members, appointed by the Under Secretary. It shall include advising the Under

Secretary on all matters related to policy, planning, execution, and evaluation of the program established under this subtitle. . . .

SEC. 346. CAPITAL AND MANAGEMENT REQUIREMENTS.

(A) CAPITAL.—(1) The private equity capital of a licensee shall be adequate to ensure a reasonable prospect that the licensee will be operated soundly and profitably, and managed actively and prudently in accordance with its articles and business plan. Such private equity capital shall not be less than $5,000,000, except that, in the case of a State sponsored licensee or a university sponsored licensee, such private equity capital shall not be less than $2,500,000.

SEC. 347. FINANCING FOR LICENSEES.

(a) AUTHORITY TO PURCHASE AND GUARANTEE PREFERRED SECURITIES.—To encourage and facilitate the formation and growth of licensees and qualified business concerns, the Under Secretary may purchase or commit to purchase nonvoting preferred securities, with or without equity warrants, issued by a licensee, or guarantee, or commit to guarantee, the payment of 100 percent of the redemption price of and dividends on such preferred securities, to the extent provided in appropriations Acts. . . . Such purchases and guarantees shall constitute direct loans and loan guarantees. . . .

(d) USE OF CAPITAL BY LICENSEES.—

(2) At least 50 percent of the amount of investments required under paragraph (1) shall be for seed and early stage financing, as defined by the Under Secretary by regulation. The Under Secretary may alter the percentage requirement under this paragraph to the extent necessary. . . .

SEC. 353. PERFORMANCE MEASURES; ANNUAL REPORT.

(a) PERFORMANCE MEASURES.—The performance of the program established under this subtitle shall be evaluated relative to progress made in achieving its purposes and shall be measured in relevant and meaningful terms such as significant accomplishments in advancing technology, businesses formed and financed, jobs created, taxes generated, licenses granted and maintained, capital invested, and other criteria the Under Secretary may deem appropriate.

(b) ANNUAL REPORT.—The Under Secretary shall prepare, in consultation with the advisory committee established under section 344, and submit annually a report to the Congress containing a full and detailed account of operations under this subtitle. Such report shall include—

(1) an assessment of progress made in achieving the purposes of this subtitle;

(2) performance measures established under subsection (a). . . .

(5) the Under Secretary's plans to ensure the provision of licensee financing to all areas of the country and to all qualified business concerns, and plans to notify and to encourage and facilitate the participation of qualified business concerns as required by section 343(e) including steps taken to accomplish those goals. . . .

SEC. 354. REPORTS, INVESTIGATIONS, AND EXAMINATIONS. . . .

(c) INVESTIGATIONS.—The Secretary may undertake investigations to determine whether a licensee or any other person has engaged or is about to engage in any acts or practices which constitute or will constitute a violation of any provision of this subtitle, or of any rule, regulation, or order issued under this subtitle. . . .

(d) EXAMINATIONS.—Each licensee shall be subject to examinations made at the discretion and direction of the Under Secretary by examiners selected or approved by, and under the supervision of, the Under Secretary. . . . The cost of such examinations, including the compensation of the examiners, may in the discretion of the Under Secretary be assessed against the licensee examined and when so assessed shall be paid by such licensee. . . .

SEC. 358. REMOVAL OR SUSPENSION OF DIRECTORS AND OFFICERS.

(a) GROUNDS.—The Secretary, after an opportunity for agency hearing, may serve upon any director or officer of a licensee a written notice of its intention to remove such director or officer from office, temporarily or permanently, whenever in the opinion of the Secretary such director or officer—

(1) has willfully and knowingly—

(A) committed any substantial violation of this subtitle or any rule, regulation, or order issued under this subtitle; or

(B) committed or engaged in any act, omission, or practice which constitutes a substantial breach of his fiduciary duty as such director or officer. . . .

TABLE B–1
SUMMARY OF H.R. 820 AND S.4,
AUTHORIZATION AS OF OCTOBER 1993
(in millions of dollars)

	H.R.820[a]		S.4[b]	
	FY 94	FY 95	FY 94	FY 95
Venture Capital Program (Title III)	1	50	2	50

a. As passed by the House on May 19, 1993.

b. As ordered reported from Senate Commerce Committee on May 25, 1993.

SOURCE: Editor.

Glenn C. Loury
Department of Economics
Boston University

Sam Peltzman
Sears Roebuck Professor of Economics
and Financial Services
University of Chicago
Graduate School of Business

Nelson W. Polsby
Professor of Political Science
University of California at Berkeley

Murray L. Weidenbaum
Mallinckrodt Distinguished
University Professor
Washington University

Research Staff

Leon Aron
Resident Scholar

Claude E. Barfield
Resident Scholar; Director, Science
and Technology Policy Studies

Walter Berns
Adjunct Scholar

Douglas J. Besharov
Resident Scholar

Jagdish Bhagwati
Visiting Scholar

Robert H. Bork
John M. Olin Scholar in Legal Studies

Michael Boskin
Visiting Scholar

Karlyn Bowman
Resident Fellow; Editor,
The American Enterprise

David Bradford
Visiting Scholar

Dick B. Cheney
Senior Fellow

Lynne V. Cheney
W.H. Brady, Jr., Distinguished Fellow

Dinesh D'Souza
John M. Olin Research Fellow

Nicholas N. Eberstadt
Visiting Scholar

Mark Falcoff
Resident Scholar

Gerald R. Ford
Distinguished Fellow

Murray F. Foss
Visiting Scholar

Suzanne Garment
Resident Scholar

Patrick Glynn
Resident Scholar

Robert A. Goldwin
Resident Scholar

Gottfried Haberler
Resident Scholar

Robert W. Hahn
Resident Scholar

Robert B. Helms
Resident Scholar

Jeane J. Kirkpatrick
Senior Fellow; Director, Foreign and
Defense Policy Studies

Marvin H. Kosters
Resident Scholar; Director,
Economic Policy Studies

Irving Kristol
John M. Olin Distinguished Fellow

Michael A. Ledeen
Resident Scholar

James Lilley
Resident Fellow; Director, Asian
Studies Program

Chong-Pin Lin
Resident Scholar; Associate Director,
Asian Studies Program

John H. Makin
Resident Scholar; Director, Fiscal
Policy Studies

Allan H. Meltzer
Visiting Scholar

Joshua Muravchik
Resident Scholar

Charles Murray
Bradley Fellow

Michael Novak
George F. Jewett Scholar in Religion,
Philosophy, and Public Policy;
Director, Social and
Political Studies

Norman J. Ornstein
Resident Scholar

Richard N. Perle
Resident Fellow

William Schneider
Resident Fellow

William Shew
Visiting Scholar

J. Gregory Sidak
Resident Scholar

Herbert Stein
Senior Fellow

Irwin M. Stelzer
Resident Scholar; Director, Regulatory
Policy Studies

Edward Styles
Director of Publications

W. Allen Wallis
Resident Scholar

Ben J. Wattenberg
Senior Fellow

Carolyn L. Weaver
Resident Scholar; Director, Social
Security and Pension Studies